LONDON BUS-TOP TOURIST

John Wittich

Copyright © J. Wittich, 1997

All Rights Reserved. No part of this publication may be reproduced, stored in a retrieval system, or transmitted in any form or by any means – electronic, mechanical, photocopying, recording, or otherwise – without prior written permission from the publisher.

Published by Sigma Leisure – an imprint of
Sigma Press, 1 South Oak Lane, Wilmslow, Cheshire SK9 6AR, England.

British Library Cataloguing in Publication Data
A CIP record for this book is available from the British Library.

ISBN: 1-85058-430-3

Typesetting and Design by: Sigma Press, Wilmslow, Cheshire.

Cover photograph: a Number 11 bus in front of the Law Courts in The Strand.

Maps and photographs: the author

Printed by: MFP Design & Print

Disclaimer: the information in this book is given in good faith and is believed to be correct at the time of publication. No responsibility is accepted by either the author or publisher for errors or omissions, or for any loss or injury howsoever caused. Only you can judge your own fitness, competence and experience.

Preface

"The best way to see London is from the top of a bus."
William Gladstone: 19th century Prime Minister

One of the delights for visitors from abroad, particularly Americans, are the double-decker buses that serve the Capital. From the "top-deck" tourists can see many of the "sights of London". But do they know where to get off the bus in order to visit them, or where the tourist spots are, or how to get to them using public transport?

I have written this book in order to help those tourists who want to know the answers to these questions. In addition to all the usual sights, the cathedrals, museums, and art galleries, I have included several trips to the lesser-known parts of London that may well be of added interest to the visitor. Some of the more popular tourist routes have "alighting points" noted in order that visitors may leave the bus and visit a selected area of tourist interest. When there are more extensive areas to explore, I have provided detailed plans or maps with, in some cases, tours on foot that are designated as "Walkabouts".

May I wish all my readers "happy hunting" in search of the sights of London.

John Wittich

Dedication

To my ever loving wife, June, who from joining me on bus trips and the careful reading of the computer script has followed this title through from beginning to end.
Thank you.

Contents

The Main Routes

Bus Route 1: Aldwych to Surrey Quays	**1**
Bus Route 2: Baker Street to Crystal Palace	**11**
Norwood Cemetery	*17*
Bus Route 11: Victoria to Liverpool Street Station	**22**
Parliament Square	*25*
Trafalgar Square Walkabout	*31*
Trafalgar Square	*33*
Covent Garden & Aldwych	*35*
Covent Garden Walkabout	*38*
The Aldwych Walkabout	*41*
St Paul's Cathedral Trail	*47*
The Bank area	*54*
Bus Route 14: Centre Point to Putney Heath	**59**
South Kensington Museums	*67*
Bus Route 15: Paddington to the Tower of London (Aldgate)	**72**
Bus Route 16: Victoria to Kilburn	**84**
Kilburn	*91*
Bus Route 24: Victoria to Hampstead Heath	**92**
Westminster Abbey	*95*
Whitehall	*98*
Highgate	*107*
Bus Route 73: Marble Arch to Stoke Newington	**109**

Short Routes to Tourist Attractions

Bus Route 11: Victoria to Chelsea	117
Bus Route 23: Paddington to Portobello Market	121
Bus Route 274: Marble Arch to London Zoo and Primrose Hill	124
Bus Route 177: Greenwich to the Thames Barrier	129
Bus Route D9: King William Street to the Isle of Dogs	131

Appendices

Appendix A: Southwark Cathedral	136
Appendix B: Attractions and Sightseeing Tours	143
Appendix C: General Information	152
Appendix D: Researching Family History	155
Appendix E: Visitorcall – The Phone Guide To London	156
Appendix F: Tourist Information Offices	157

Index   158

Bus Route 1: Aldwych to Surrey Quays

Route   Aldwych – Strand – Lancaster Place – Waterloo Bridge – Tenison Way – Waterloo Road – St George's Circus – Elephant and Castle – New Kent Road – Tower Bridge Road – Grange Road – Southwark Park Road – Galleywell Road – New Road – Surrey Quays.

Start   Aldwych

Finish   Surrey Quays

Time   Allow sixty minutes for the journey.

Bus No.   1

Return   Either by No. 1 or by a single-decker bus from outside the shopping centre.

Tickets   To cover Zones 1 & 2.

Aldwych was once one of the worst slum areas in London. The present road layout was built in the early twentieth century and was officially opened on 18th October 1905 by King Edward VII and Queen Alexandra. The king cut the tape and legend records that he forgot his words and had to be prompted! Several side streets were swept away to make the "new" broad thoroughfare of Kingsway that links High Holborn with the Strand. At the end of Kingsway is **Bush House** which was built to the designs of an American architect, Harvey W. Corbett, and completed in 1935. The original intention was to have a vast, luxurious, shopping showpiece here with an arcade of shops leading from Kingsway to the Strand on the other side of the building. These plans never came to fruition. Instead, in 1940 the British Broadcasting Corporation (BBC), needing more office and studio space for their expanding overseas services, leased much of the building. They are still there today and over the years Bush House has become synonymous with the BBC's External Radio Services.

Opposite Bush House is **St Catherine's House**, the home of the Registrar General and the central office for the registration of births, marriages and deaths for England and Wales. A useful source when researching a family tree. Find the bus stop and board a No. 1 bus.

At the end of the Aldwych, on the right-hand side, is Australia House, the office of the Australian Commission. Built between 1912 and 1918, it was designed by Messrs. Marshall Mackenzie and A.G.R. Mackenzie. George V laid the foundation stone in 1913, and officially opened the offices in 1918. The site was previously occupied by the Victoria State Building. This has been incorporated into the present building. The sculptures at the entrance are by H. Palmer and represent exploration and agriculture, on the cornice are the Horses of the Sun by Bertram Mackennal.

Opposite is the RAF Church of **St Clement Danes** in front of which stands three statues. In front is the bronze of William Gladstone, by Hamo Thornycroft, which shows him in his robes as Chancellor of the Exchequer. Around the base are four reliefs depicting Brotherhood, Aspiration, Education and Courage. Behind are statues of Lord Dowding, the Scottish Air Force Chief, and "Bomber" Harris, Commander in Chief of the RAF Bomber Command. Both served during the Second World War. The church was originally built by the Danes who were allowed to settle here, outside the City Walls. On his death in 1040, Harold I, also known as Harold Harefoot, son of King Canute and Aelgifu, was first buried in Westminster Abbey. Later he was resurrected by his Danish relatives and buried with honour in the churchyard here. The location of the grave is unknown. The church is dedicated to St Clement, an early Bishop of Rome, who suffered death for his faith by being tied to a ship's anchor and thrown overboard while the ship was at sea. It seems appropriate that the Danes should choose St Clement, being a sea-faring race themselves. After the Great Fire of 1666, Christopher Wren rebuilt the church, but the spire was added later by James Gibbs. The building was severely damaged during the Second World War, and after restoration was given over to the Royal Air Force as their Central Church.

Next the parish church of **St Mary le Strand** stands on an island in the middle of the roadway on the right-hand side. It was designed by the Scottish, Catholic architect, James Gibbs, and was consecrated on 1st January 1724. The church has been described as the finest Baroque church in England by a number of leading architectural historians. It stands on its island amidst the busy traffic of the Strand and yet it can be one of the most peaceful churches in London. Much of Gibbs's later reputation stems from his work on this church. It was his first public building in London and reflects the strong influence of Carlo Fontana, his tutor in Rome. It was originally planned to erect a 250ft column surmounted by a statue of Queen Anne at the west end of the church. However, the Queen died and a steeple was placed on the west tower instead! The brass statue's whereabouts are unknown, it was made by John Talman in Florence, but there is no record that it ever arrived in this country. A stone statue of the Queen, now standing on a pedestal in Queen Anne's Gate near St James's Park Station, is often pointed out as being the statue. But is it? Today, in addition to being a parish church, with a lively church school in Drury Lane, it serves as the Central Church of the former Women's Royal Naval Service (WReNS) now the Women's Royal Navy. Charles Dickens's parents were married here in 1809, and Bonnie Prince Charles was here received into the Church of England in 1750. During the road widening of the Strand in 1872 the churchyard was abolished and a footpath constructed round the church.

On the left is **King's College**, part of the University of London.

The George public house in The Strand

It was founded in 1828 to counter the godless **University College** in Gower Street. "Godless" colleges had been founded to cater for non-members of the Established Church (of England) who, at that time, were excluded from attending either Oxford or Cambridge. The original University College was set up as a Company Limited with articles forbidding the building of any place of worship on the site. Since 1846, when the Theological Department was set up, King's has become a major centre for the training of priests for the Church of England.

Next to the college is **Somerset House,** first built in the sixteenth century by Protector Somerset who did not live to see its completion. He was executed for being "over ambitious" in his task of looking after the young King Edward VI. In the following century it became the royal residence for the Catholic Queen Henrietta Maria, Charles I's wife, who had a chapel built here for Roman Catholic services. Several of the Queen's attendants are buried in the vaults beneath the great square. (The burial vaults are not open to members of the public.) Here Inigo Jones, the Palladian architect, died, and Oliver Cromwell's body lay in state. The old house was destroyed in 1775 and the present building, by William Chambers, was erected in its place. The east wing is now occupied by King's College, and the State Rooms have been restored and now house the paintings of the Courtauld Institute of Art. They are well worth a visit!

Lancaster Place leads to Waterloo Bridge. On the right is Brettenham House, built in 1932 by W.E. Hunt, which houses the office of the Duchy of Lancaster. The Duchy consists of a number of estates amounting to some 21000 hectares (52,000 acres) that are the private property of the Duke of Lancaster. The Dukedom is always held by the reigning monarch, hence the Queen is acknowledged here as the Duke. When the nearby Chapel of the Savoy sings the National Anthem, the last line becomes "God save the Duke".

From Waterloo Bridge, a wide vista of the City of London can be seen on the left-hand side. The bridge, designed by Sir Giles Gilbert Scott, was formally opened on the 10th of December 1945 by Herbert Morrison, Home Secretary in Winston Churchill's wartime government. The first bridge was designed by George Dodd, built by John Rennie and opened 18th June 1817, the second anniversary of the Battle of Waterloo – hence its name. Canova, the Italian sculptor wrote, "It is the noblest bridge in the world, and worth a visit from

Waterloo Bridge from South Bank

the remotest corners of the earth." However, some hundred years later the bridge began to sink and after much heated discussion it was agreed to demolish it and commission a new one – in 1938. Work on the bridge continued throughout the Second World War. It was finally completed in November 1944. Girders from the temporary bridge that had been erected alongside the former bridge were then used to form a bridge across the River Rhine in Germany and so aided the advance of the Allied Troops.

At the "south" end of the bridge, on the left-hand side, can be seen **The Royal National Theatre** which was designed by Sir Denis Lasdun. In 1976 the National Theatre Company moved into its new and final home. The idea for a National Theatre, based in London, was first proposed in 1848 by Effingham Wilson – a London publisher. Over the ensuing years other proposals were brought forward. In the 1930s a site was purchased in Cromwell Road, opposite the Victoria and Albert Museum, but the outbreak of the Second World War in 1939 put a stop to all building plans for the theatre. During the Festival of Britain in 1951, Her Majesty Queen Elizabeth, now the Queen Mother, laid the foundation for a theatre on South Bank.

The theatre was formally opened in 1976 by Queen Elizabeth the Second. The original foundation stone reads:

"To the living memory of William Shakespeare on a site provided by the London County Council in conformity with the National Theatre Act of MCMXLIX and in the year of the Festival of Britain This foundation stone for The National Theatre was laid on XIII July MCMLI by Her Majesty the Queen."

On the right-hand side can be seen the **Royal Festival Hall**. Built as part of the Festival of Britain, it was designed by Sir Robert Matthew and J.L. Martin with later additions by Sir Hubert Bennet. The main hall is used for a variety of artistic purposes from solo recitals to full length ballets.

St John's Church, Waterloo Road was designed by Francis Bedford and built on piles over the Lambeth Marsh between 1822 and 1824. Gutted in December 1940, it was restored by T.F. Ford as part of the Festival of Britain. It was then used by all denominations of the Christian Church. The wall paintings are by Hans Feibusch. The late Sir John Summerson, sometime curator of the Soane Museum in Lincoln's Inn once wrote " *the tower is the kind that Ictinus might have put on the Parthenon, if the Athenians had had the advantage of belonging to the Church of England"*.

Waterloo Station was opened in 1848 as a result of extending the railway tracks of the London and South Western Railway Company from their previous terminal at Nine Elms (Vauxhall). The track lies on a curved brick viaduct over the Lambeth Marsh and consists of 290 arches. Between 1907 and 1922 the station buildings were entirely rebuilt. Pevsner records it as being, " *the only 20th century station building in London with architectural ambitions."*. In the 1990s a new addition was made to the station with the building of a terminal for the Channel Tunnel train service.

On the corner of The Cut and Waterloo Road is **The Old Vic Theatre**, which was built in 1818 and originally named the Royal Coburg Theatre after its patrons, Prince Leopold and Princess Charlotte. In 1881 it became a Temperance Theatre for the working class. The social reformer and first lady member of the former London County Council, Emma Cons, took over the running of the theatre. In 1898 she was joined by her niece, Lillian Baylis, who, after her aunt's death in 1912, took over the theatre. By the third decade of the twentieth century, The Old Vic had become one of London's leading theatres, with popular priced seats offering operas and Shakespearean plays. In 1935, with the building of the Sadlers Wells Theatre in Rosebery Avenue, Finsbury, opera and ballet were transferred to the new theatre. The Old Vic continued to offer Shakespeare. After an extensive rebuilding programme in 1963, it reopened as the first, temporary, home for the National Theatre Company under the direction of Sir Laurence Olivier.

Opposite The Old Vic is Lower Marsh Road with its daily street market. Waterloo Road continues to St George's Circus where six busy thoroughfares meet. From here it is possible to reach the river bridges of Blackfriars, Waterloo and Westminster. In the centre of the roadway once stood an obelisk that was later moved to the grounds of the Royal Bethlem Hospital for the Mentally ill, it is now the Imperial War Museum in Lambeth Road. On the three sides of the obelisk are recorded the distances to Fleet Street, Westminster Hall and London Bridge. In its new place these distances are inaccurate. When it stood here it was known to the young Charles Dickens who visited a shop "close by the obelisk" when he took his father's clothes to be valued. His father, John, had been committed to the Marshalsea Prison for debts and it was " *a condition that a debtor had to disclose all wearable effects of himself and family before the official appraiser in the matter of his bankruptcy*", wrote his biographer, John Forster. Dickens used the obelisk in his story of David Copperfield, who had his trunk taken from him here in the pretence of carrying it to the Dover Stage. The whole area was once known as St George's Fields and was often used for illegal gatherings. In the 1780s they were the setting for the massing of the Gordon Rioters, who then went on the rampage chanting, "No Popery".

London Road leads to the Elephant and Castle district. Historians differ on the origin of the name. One school of thought favours the Infanta of Castille, a daughter of the King and Queen of Portugal or Spain, thereby honouring Catherine of Aragon and Castille, the wife of Prince Arthur, and later of Henry VIII. The alternative school favours the elephant that always carries a castle (houdah) on its back. These animals were used for tiger hunting, when the hunter would be safely ensconced in his castle/houdah. The Worshipful Company of Cutlers of the City of London's crest is an elephant with a castle on its back. Elephants' tusks were often used for the handles of cutlery.

Alexander Fleming House, on the left, was designed by the world famous architect Erno Goldfinger for the, then, Ministry of Health in the 1960s. It is named after the discoverer of penicillin, Sir Alexander Fleming. The building has now become a listed (protected) building as a construction of historical interest and architectural merit.

The centrepiece on the island of the roundabout hides the electricity sub-station for the underground railway here. It is also hailed as a memorial to Michael Faraday, who was born nearby. The discovery of electromagnetic induction led to the development of the electric motor and dynamo.

On the far side of the roundabout can be seen the six-columned portico of the **Metropolitan Tabernacle** which was built in 1861, at a cost of £30,000, for the ever popular Reverend Charles Spurgeon, a Baptist minister. On his death in 1892 he left fifty volumes of sermons, a collection of pithy sayings and a number of other works. He regularly preached to congregations of seven thousand or more in number. A theological college named after him can be found on South Norwood Hill, London SE25.

New Kent Road was first laid out in the mid-eighteenth century and was designed to link the Old Kent Road to St George's Road at a time when the area was being developed. On either side of the road can be seen a much later development, with the housing estates having been erected in the post-war years. The work was carried out as part of the Elephant and Castle Improvement Scheme under the direction of the former London County Council.

Just after Falmouth Road, on the left, can be seen the **David Copperfield Gardens**. The memorial in the gardens was erected by the Dickens Fellowship in 1932. It commemorates David Copperfield pausing here after chasing the long-legged young man who had robbed him of his trunk and money.

Immediately before the flyover that links the Old and New Kent Roads stands the St Saviour and St Olave Grammar School buildings.

Tower Bridge Road leads to one of London's most famous bridges across the River Thames and was once a boundary between the Boroughs of Southwark and Bermondsey. Today the two former boroughs have been combined with a third (Camberwell) to form the much larger London Borough of Southwark. Many of the street names along this part of the route are reminders of days gone by. Grange Road marks the site of a series of large barns in which the monks of the Abbey of Bermondsey stored their produce.

Bermondsey Spa (Park) recalls the days when the citizens of London and elsewhere could flock to drink the pure waters of the Spa here. An eighteenth century pamphlet described the Spa thus:

"We found the entrance presents a vista between trees, hung with lamps, blue, red, green and white; nor is the walk in which they are hung inferior (length excepted) to the Grand Walk in Vauxhall Gardens... The accommodations at this place on a Sunday are very good and the charges reasonable... This elegant place of entertainment is situated in the lower road, between the Borough of Southwark and Deptford" Besant, South London. 1898.

Southwark Park Road leads to the park, but just before the railway bridge the bus turns to the right along Galleywall Road. Rotherhithe New Road follows, ending our journey at Surrey Quays underground station. From the terminus it is a short walk to the Surrey Quays Shopping Centre. Built on the site of the Surrey Commercial Docks that were originally known as the Howland Great Wet Dock, part of the dock has been retained and forms a pleasant watery oasis – Canada Water – to sit and rest. Canada is a pleasant reminder of the dock's past when much trade was carried out with that country. Here can be seen a variety of wetland habitats. An illustrated diorama near the wind-pump clearly explains the inhabitants of the water, both fowl and flora.

Before returning back to central London and by taking another short walk, the pleasures of Southwark Park can be enjoyed. The entrance is a short walk from the bus stop near the underground station. Southwark Park was for many years a misnomer because, prior to the reorganisation of the Boroughs of London in 1965, the park was in the former Borough of Bermondsey. It was opened to the public in 1869, at a cost of £50,000, and offers 27 hectares (66 acres) of unrivalled facilities for sport and recreation. In addition there are a number of fine trees to admire while rockeries and massed flower beds add to the pleasure for its visitors.

For the journey back to central London, return to the bus stop by the underground station and board a number 188. The route, along Lower Road, passes the Park and St Olave's Hospital. The hospital has the reputation of being one of the busiest in London, and has served the neighbourhood for the past two hundred years. At the end of the road there is a roundabout. Look to the right and see the entrance to the **Rotherhithe Tunnel** that links Rotherhithe with Shadwell on the opposite bank of the river. It was built between 1904 and 1908 to the designs of Sir Maurice Fitzmaurice. In order to allow the passage of large ships on the way to the Pool of London, the top of the tunnel is 48ft below the Trinity high-water mark.

Next to the tunnel entrance is the Norwegian Church of St Olave with its weathervane designed like a Viking ship.

During the laying out of the roadway system some 3,000 people had to be rehoused. Jamaica Road, that leads us towards London Bridge, is named after the old Jamaica Tavern – visited in the seventeenth century by the diarist, Samuel Pepys. He would come to the riverside Cherry Garden: *"and so to the Cherry Garden, and then by water singing finely to the Bridge, and there landed: so took boat again, and to Somerset House." (Diary, 15th June 1664.)*

The road continues to Tower Bridge Road where the bus turns left and soon reaches The Bricklayers Arms roundabout. Once more the Paragon Gardens, noted on the outward journey, can be seen on the left-hand side of the road as the route takes us back along the New Kent Road. We leave the Elephant and Castle roundabout by way of St George's Road where the obelisk that used to stand in St George's Circus can be seen. It now stands on the edge of Geraldine Mary Harmsworth Park. When the Royal Bethlem Hospital was moved to Addington, Surrey in 1930, the grounds were purchased by Lord Rothermere and given to the London County Council in memory of his mother – Geraldine Mary Harmsworth. It was originally founded in 1247 and lays claim to being the oldest establishment of its kind in Europe. In 1936 part of the hospital was demolished and the remainder used to house the Imperial War Museum.

Opposite the park is the Roman Catholic **Cathedral of St George**. Designed by Augustus Welby Northmore Pugin in 1841, its west tower is still incomplete while the interior has been completely rebuilt after extensive damage during the Second World War. From the cathedral, the Lambeth Road leads back to St George's Circus, Waterloo Road, over Waterloo Bridge (to the left can be seen the Houses of Parliament), along Lancaster Place and finally crossing the Strand to the Aldwych where our journey began.

Bus Route 2: Baker Street to Crystal Palace

Route Baker Street – Portman Square – Orchard Street – Oxford Street – Park Lane – Hyde Park Corner – Grosvenor Place – Lower Grosvenor Place – Buckingham Palace Road – Grosvenor Gardens – Terminus Place – Vauxhall Bridge Road – Bessborough Gardens – Vauxhall Bridge – Vauxhall Cross – South Lambeth Road – Stockwell – Stockwell Road – Brixton Road – Effra Road – Tulse Hill – Norwood Road – Norwood High Street – Elder Road – Central Hill – Westow Hill – Crystal Palace Parade.

Start Baker Street, Marylebone

Finish Crystal Palace Parade, Sydenham

Time Allow sixty minutes for the journey.

Bus No. 2

Return Either by No.2 bus or from British Rail Station on Annerley Hill.

Tickets Travelcard covering Zones 1 to 4.

Although the No. 2 bus terminus is Great Central Street, close to Marylebone (BR) Station, it is easier to board it at Bus Stop F outside number 120 Baker Street. Check the destination of the bus as during certain parts of the day the No.2 from here goes only as far as West Norwood Garage, where another No. 2 will complete the journey.

To many people Baker Street is synonymous with Sherlock Holmes, Doctor Watson and 221B Baker Street, the latter a number that did not exist during the lifetime of their creator, Sir Arthur Conan Doyle. In the nineteenth century, when the duo "lived" at 221B, the street's numbering stopped at 84. The upper portion of the street being then called Upper York Place.

Shortly after leaving the bus stop, the Sherlock Holmes Hotel can be seen on the left-hand side. Regular meetings, dinners and functions of the Sherlock Holmes Society are held here. On the right-hand side is the head office of Marks & Spencer, here is the true site of 221B Baker Street. This was identified in a letter by Conan Doyle to a friend as being the house and shop that he had in mind when writing the stories. It was lived in at the time by friends of the author and, in order not to embarrass them, he changed the number to an imaginary one – 221B.

At the end of the street is **Portman Square** which was laid out in the late eighteenth century for the ground landlord Henry Portman. It is one of London's best kept private squares and access is allowed to key-holders only. These are persons who either live in the houses or work in the offices and who pay an annual sum towards the maintenance of the gardens. Number 20, in the north-west corner, was designed by the Scottish architect Robert Adams.

Leading out of the square is Orchard Street, recalling another of the Portman Estates – Orchard Portman, near Taunton, in Somerset. Oxford Street is at the end of the street, and after turning to the right, the bus arrives at **Marble Arch**. The arch, a memorial to Lord Nelson, the famous English admiral who was shot at the Battle of Trafalgar, once stood at the entrance to Buckingham Palace. It was designed by John Nash, George IV's favourite architect, and is based on the Arch of Constantine in Rome. A statue of George IV by Sir Francis Chantry, now standing in Trafalgar Square, was originally intended for the top of the arch.

Hyde Park is now on the right-hand side of the roadway as the bus moves down Park Lane. Here can be seen, on the left, three of London's most famous hotels: Grosvenor House, The Dorchester and The London Hilton. **Grosvenor House Hotel** stands on the site of Gloucester House, the London home of George III's brother, the Duke of Gloucester. It was later occupied by Robert Grosvenor, 2nd Earl Grosvenor, from whom the hotel takes its name. The hotel was the first to include a swimming pool among its amenities that, between 1929 and 1934, also included a skating rink. In addition to over four hundred bedrooms, the complex also has a block of a hundred and fifty luxury flats.

The Dorchester Hotel is on the site of a large house which was erected in 1751 for Joseph Damer. In 1792 Damer became the Earl of Dorchester. In 1928 Sir Robert McAlpine and Gordon Hotels Ltd bought the house and demolished it. The present building, designed by William Curtis Green, was opened in April 1931. Extensions were added in 1952, with a suite of rooms designed by Oliver Messel. There are now nearly three hundred bedrooms in the hotel. The suite of rooms used by General Eisenhower during the Second World War has been restored to reproduce its condition during his occupation.

The London Hilton is thirty storeys high and commands fine views from many of its rooms overlooking the park and the western side of London. Opened in 1963, the architects were Lewis Solomon, Kaye and Partners. It has over five hundred rooms.

Hyde Park Corner is the busiest road junction in London and is the meeting place of five of the Capital's major roadways: Park Lane, Piccadilly, Constitution Hill, Grosvenor Place and Knightsbridge. One side of the junction is dominated by **Apsley House**, once known as Number One, London. It was designed by Robert Adam and lived in by the first Duke of Wellington – the hero of the Battle of Waterloo. Today it forms the Wellington Museum and contains many interesting items relating to the Duke and his life. The house is open every day except Mondays from 11am to 5pm. There is an admission charge.

On the road island can be seen the Wellington Arch and the Royal Regiment of Artillery War Memorial. **The Wellington Arch**, designed by Decimus Burton, was erected in 1828 as a memorial to the Duke of Wellington whose equestrian statue was placed on top. This was later removed to an Army parade ground in Aldershot, Hampshire, and the present Quadriga group was erected in 1912. This was paid for by the Jewish financier Lord Michelham in memory of his friend, Edward VII. **The Royal Regiment of Artillery War Memorial**, designed by C. Sargeant Jagger, has a series of interesting reliefs including a Virgin and Child around its pedestal. These are by Lionel Pearson. If the field gun on the top of the memorial were capable of being fired, the shell would fall into the area of the Battle of the Somme, the place where so many gunners lost their lives in the First World War.

Standing opposite Apsley House, now the Wellington Museum, are statues of Wellington and David. The Duke of Wellington is depicted astride "Copenhagen", his favourite horse, with four soldier figures, one on each corner, representing the 1st Guards and 42nd Royal Highlanders on the north side, and the 23rd Royal Welsh Fusiliers and the 6th Inniskilling Dragoons on the south side. With his back towards the end of Park Lane, stands the naked figure of

David, holding a sword in the left-hand and supported, either side on the plinth, by machine guns. It is the War Memorial of the Machine Gun Corps and previously stood at Stanhope Gate in Hyde Park, opposite the Dorchester Hotel.

The road, Grosvenor Place, follows the wall of Buckingham Palace round to Buckingham Palace Road where shortly afterwards it enters the lower half of Grosvenor Gardens. Here, on the right, is the equestrian statue to Marshall Foch, soldier and Marshall of France, by G. Mallisard. The public gardens here are shaped as fleur-de-lys in honour of France.

Terminus Place, by the forecourt of the railway and bus station, also has a bus stop for the No.2, after which the bus enters Vauxhall Bridge Road. On the way it passes **"Little Ben"**, a 9 metres (30ft) edition of St Stephen's Clock tower that is part of the Houses of Parliament. It was returned here in 1981 after being removed during road-widening in the 1960s. A French oil company paid for its restoration to commemorate the wedding in 1981 of the Prince and Princess of Wales.

As the bus travels down Vauxhall Bridge Road, **The Apollo Theatre** can be seen on the right. This was originally the New Victoria Cinema which was built in 1929 and designed by Trent and Lewis. This is followed by the Queen Mother Sports Centre which was opened in 1980 by the Queen Mother herself. Another part of the Post-War development of the area is the Lillington Estate with its red brick houses and flats. In the middle of the estate stands the parish church of St James the Less by George Edmund Street. Once described as being "like a lily among weeds", it now matches the surrounding buildings.

At the end of the road, before it passes over the bridge, is the stop for those wishing to visit **The Tate Gallery** on Millbank. From the bridge, on the left-hand side, can be seen the sweep of the river towards the Houses of Parliament, and the offices along the south bank. The green and yellow building at the foot of the bridge is the new home of the "Secret Services" of Great Britain. Passing under the railway bridge and Vauxhall Railway Station and turning right, the bus enters South Lambeth Road. On the left is Vauxhall Park, all that is left of the once famous Vauxhall Pleasure Gardens of the eighteenth century, after which the townscape, houses, shops and flats present a cosmopolitan collection of buildings from the nineteenth and twentieth centuries.

At Stockwell there is a Memorial Clock Tower and a solid-looking concrete structure left over from the last war. It covers the shaft that leads deep below the surface of the ground to tunnels that were built to accommodate Londoners should there have been an atomic war. Today they are used for storage of archival papers.

Stockwell Road leads to Brixton which has one of the most cosmopolitan populations of any in the Capital. Here live Cypriots, Maltese, Chileans, Vietnamese, Asians, Africans and Caucasians in joyful harmony. Shops abound, and everybody with a liking for street markets should alight here to visit Electric Avenue's market. The avenue takes its name from the fact that it was the first street in South London to be lit with electricity. This enabled the market stallholders to encourage late night shopping.

Ahead can be seen the parish church of **St Matthew**, built in 1822. It was one of the "Waterloo Churches" built as a thank offering after the Battle of Waterloo. It was designed by William Porden, but only the exterior of his church remains. In recent times the interior has been completely revamped to accommodate a community centre, with the crypt being used for theatrical performances. Opposite the church stands Lambeth Town Hall, the centre of administration for the London Borough of Lambeth since 1964. The building was declared officially open by George V and Queen Mary in 1908, while they were still the Prince and Princess of Wales.

Effra Road, to the left of the church, runs along the line of the local River Effra, which at the time of Elizabeth I was navigable from Brixton to the River Thames by Lambeth Bridge. It has long been one of London's lost rivers. The road itself is a mixture of houses, light industrial buildings and flats leading to Tulse Hill. Half way up the hill, on the left-hand side, is St Martin-in-the-Fields High School for Girls. This was founded by the famous church in Trafalgar Square in 1699 as a charity school in the parish. It was moved here in 1928 and was opened by the Queen Mother, then the Duchess of York.

Norwood Road follows from Tulse Hill and shortly the parish church of St Luke's, West Norwood can be seen – another of the "Waterloo Churches". Alight from the bus here, by the Thurlow Arms public house, and walk along to the fine wrought-iron gates

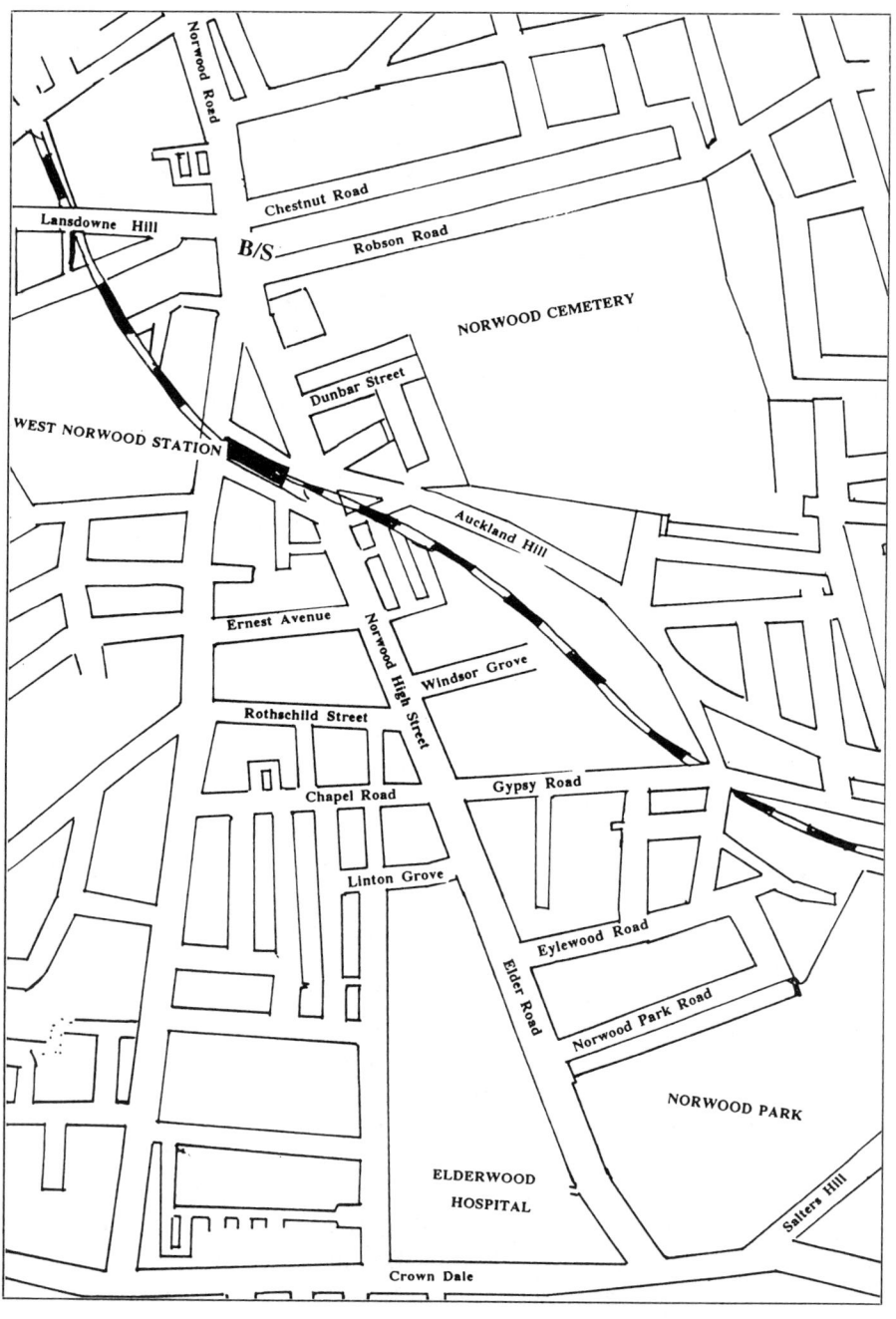

of the South Metropolitan Cemetery and the **West Norwood Crematorium**. Founded in 1837 by the South Metropolitan Cemetery Company, the cemetery covers 16 hectares (39 acres) and contains a number of interesting graves of famous people. It was designed by Sir William Tite, the architect of the Royal Exchange in the City and numerous railway stations. A high wall surrounds the grounds in order to prevent body-snatchers from carrying out their illegal, but profitable business. Tite's other cemetery is at Brookwood, near Woking in Surrey. For the classical student or scholar there is a section of the cemetery devoted to the Brotherhood of the Greek Community in London of 1842. A fair number of Germans are buried here due to there once being a German Church near Forest Hill. In the south-east corner there is a plot reserved for the parishioners of the Wren church of St Mary-at-Hill in the City. In 1966 Lambeth Council took over the control of the cemetery and is now responsible for its maintenance. A wander round the cemetery can be a very enlightening experience! Here lie buried: architects, engineers, composers, men of finance, shopkeepers and many other trades and professions. There is even a Polish-born juggler and clown.

Norwood Cemetery: key to map (see next page)

1. **Peter Cow:** Inventor of Cow rubber products.
2. **Henry Tate:** Public benefactor and inventor of the sugar cube. His collection of paintings formed the basis for the gallery he built on Millbank – The Tate Gallery.
3. **Charles Spurgeon:** A popular Baptist preacher of the nineteenth century whose congregation built him the Metropolitan Tabernacle at the Elephant and Castle.
4. **Henry Doulton:** A potter who, after entering the family business in Lambeth, developed graffito ware – "a technique in mural ceramic decoration in which the top layer of glaze, plaster, etc., is incised with a design to reveal parts of the ground".
5. **Mrs Beeton:** Author of the famous "Mrs Beeton's Household Management" a 'must for every newly wedded bride!'. Contrary to popular belief, she did not say "take ten eggs" or "first catch your hare". The purpose of her original book was to show brides, and others, the basics of household management. Her son, Sir Mayson Beeton, wrote to *The Daily Mail* and stated, "Its chief object was to promote efficiency and economy in the household."

6 William Marsden: The surgeon who founded the Royal Free Hospital in Hampstead in 1828. It was originally known as "The London General Institution for the Gratuitous Care of Malignant Diseases" and the poor could receive treatment without payment. Marsden was walking through Holborn one day and found a dying girl on the steps of St Andrew Holborn Church. She had been unable to find a subscriber to the local hospital to recommend her, and so was dying in the street. Marsden also founded the Brompton Cancer Hospital in Fulham Road.

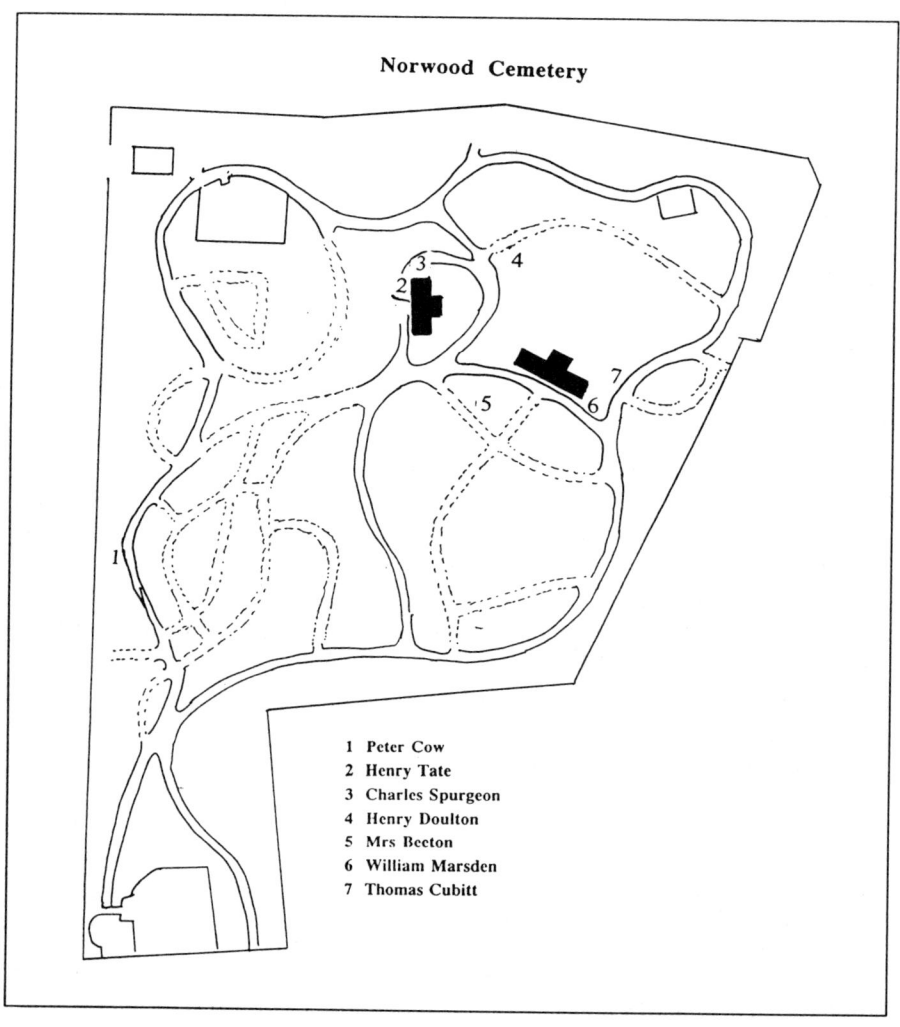

Norwood Cemetery

1 Peter Cow
2 Henry Tate
3 Charles Spurgeon
4 Henry Doulton
5 Mrs Beeton
6 William Marsden
7 Thomas Cubitt

7   **Thomas Cubitt:** A builder who rebuilt "half of London" in the nineteenth century, including the front of Buckingham Palace. He was a guarantor for the Great Exhibition of 1851.

St Luke's parish church is the fourth and last of the "Waterloo Churches" that can be found in the Lambeth area. Unlike the other three, this church was built by a female building contractor – Elizabeth Broomfield. Its architect was Francis Bedford, who also produced St John's church in Waterloo Road, and it was erected between 1822 and 1825. One great advantage this building has over the other three is its elevated position. The interior was remodelled by George Edmund Street in the 1870s, in the Romanesque style of Italy of the eleventh century.

Norwood High Street passes alongside the church and leads to Elder Road, with **Norwood Park** on its left-hand side. The park covers some 13 hectares (33 acres) and owes its existence mainly to the generosity of Sir Ernest Tritton who was the Member of Parliament for Norwood from 1892 to 1906.

At the junction with Central Hill, the road starts the climb up to Crystal Palace Parade, on the way passing the Roman Catholic Virgo Fidelis Independent Day School for Girls, with a Catholic church within its grounds. On the way look out for the period houses on the right-hand side of the roadway dating from the nineteenth century. As the bus ascends the hill, keep an eye out to the left. Between the buildings or down the side streets there are glimpses of the City of London in the distance. Here, too, are shops with living quarters above which have much to offer the visitor at the end of their journey. The White Swan public house on the left-hand side marks the end of Crystal Palace Parade and our journey from Baker Street to the **Crystal Palace.**

Originally built for the Great Exhibition of 1851 in Hyde Park, the vast glasshouse was dismantled at the end of the exhibition and rebuilt here in 1854. In 1936, whether by accident or design, a fire destroyed most of the building, and bombing in the Second World War added to the damage. During the First World War, 1914-1918, the buildings and grounds were used as a training centre for men of the Royal Navy. It is said that it was not an unusual sight to see sailors in town with their caps bearing the insignia *HMS Crystal*

Megalosaurus

Palace. Today, caps bearing the words Crystal Palace indicate the presence of supporters of the local football team!

Before leaving, take some time to explore the grounds, they are full of interest both ancient and modern. In one corner of the park is a Dinosaur Theme Park, the brainchild of Professor Richard Owen, the eminent palaeontologist. With the support of Prince Albert he built life-sized monsters. Here can be seen, but not touched, the Megatherium, Pterodactylus and the Teleosaurus, not forgetting the mammal-like reptiles the Dicynodonts, and a few more too. The whole display was opened by Queen Victoria in June 1854. From here there is a splendid view across the valley to the North Downs in one direction, and the Thames Valley, including the City of London, in the other.

Bus Route 2: Baker Street to Crystal Palace

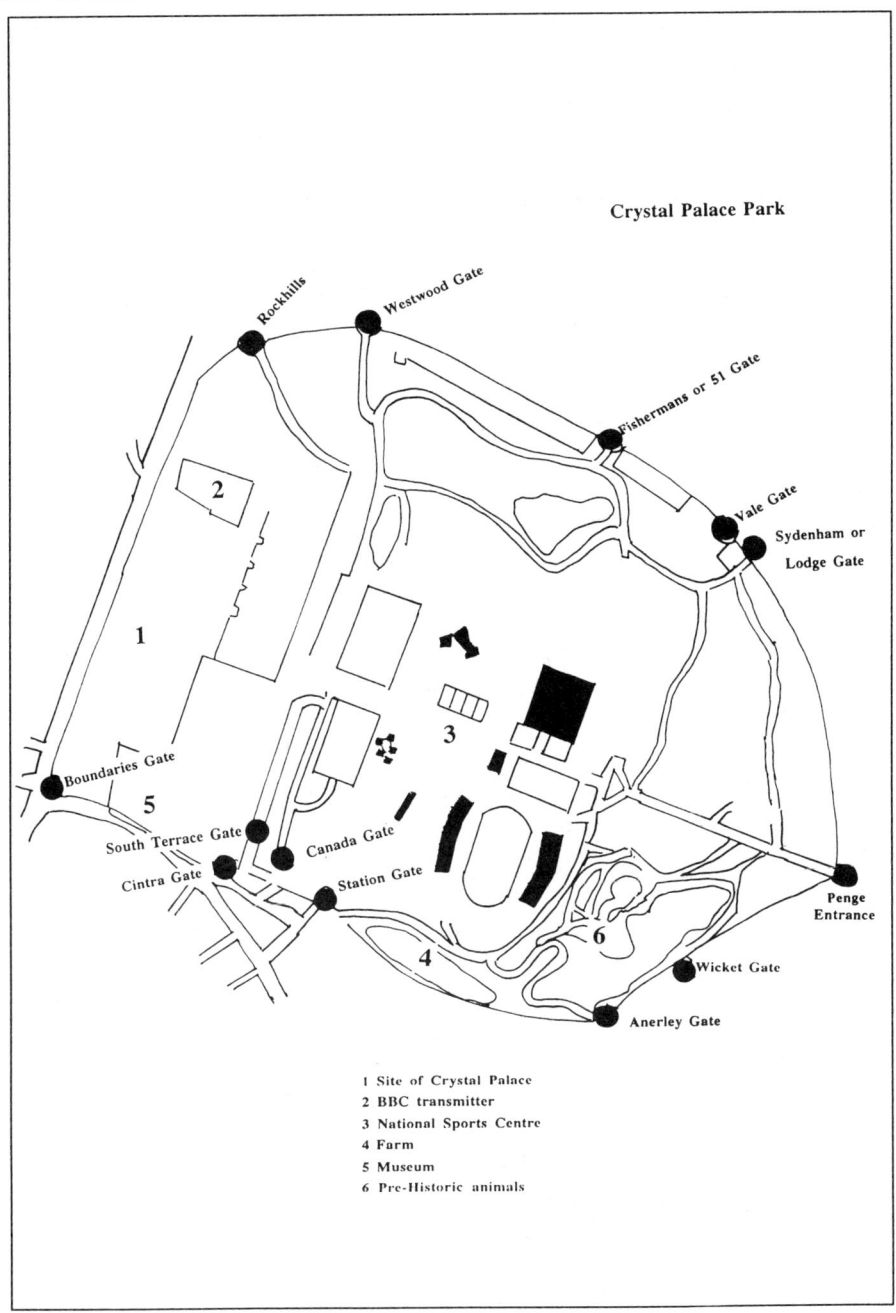

Crystal Palace Park

1 Site of Crystal Palace
2 BBC transmitter
3 National Sports Centre
4 Farm
5 Museum
6 Pre-Historic animals

Bus Route 11: Victoria to Liverpool Street Station

Route Victoria Station – Victoria Street – Parliament Square – Houses of Parliament – Whitehall – Downing Street – Trafalgar Square – Duncannon Street – *Walkabout* – Strand – Aldwych – W*alkabout* - Covent Garden – Strand – Fleet Street – Ludgate Hill – Cannon Street – Queen Victoria Street – The Bank – Liverpool Street Station.

Start Terminus Place, forecourt of Victoria Station.

Finish Liverpool Street Station, City of London.

Time Allow forty-five to fifty minutes for the journey.

Bus No. 11

Return Either by the No. 11 bus or by the underground railway.

Tickets Travelcard to cover Zones 1 & 2.

Terminus Place, sandwiched between the underground station and the bus station at Victoria, is the starting place for our tour on the No. 11 bus. When leaving the station area, the bus negotiates the one-way system for traffic emerging into Victoria Street. The street was built in the last century as part of a redevelopment plan to ease the flow of traffic from Westminster in a westward direction.

Shortly, on the right-hand side of the road, with its piazza in front, proudly stands **Westminster Cathedral.** In 1850 a Roman Catholic hierarchy was reinstated in England and Nicholas Wiseman was appointed by the Pope, Pius IX, to be the first Archbishop of Westminster. It was not until 1884 that the Roman Catholic Church was able to buy the site where the cathedral now stands. The foundation stone was laid by Cardinal Vaughan, the third Archbishop in 1895. Designed by John Francis Bentley, the style chosen is Byzantine in order that worshippers and others should not confuse this building with Westminster Abbey at the other end of the street – but they still do!

The west front of Westminster Cathedral

On the corner of Victoria Street and Buckingham Gate stands The Albert public house with its first floor restaurant dominated by portraits of Victorian Prime Ministers of Great Britain. Its proximity to the Houses of Parliament makes it a popular rendezvous for members of both the House of Commons (the Lower House) and the House of Lords (the Upper House). There is a "division bell" in the restaurant that is used to recall members of both Houses when their presence is required for voting.

A green open space on the left-hand side marks the spot of a former churchyard, the church itself was severely damaged in the last war and not rebuilt. The churchyard was a plague pit during the Great Plague of 1665 and has never been built on. It is said to have been the burial place of Captain Blood, the "gentleman" who attempted to steal the crown jewels of England from the Tower of London in the seventeenth century. The multi-windowed building just past the former churchyard is the home of the Metropolitan

Police – **Scotland Yard**. Originally founded in Scotland Yard, off Whitehall, the Force moved here in 1967. This is their third headquarters building and was designed by Chapman Taylor and Partners. It covers 4 hectares (11 acres) and has nearly seven hundred rooms including the notorious "Black Museum". The museum houses many macabre mementos of crimes committed in the Metropolitan area, but, alas, it is not open to the public.

At the end of Victoria Street is Broad Sanctuary and **Westminster Abbey**. Up to the time of the English Reformation in the sixteenth century there were a number of "sanctuaries" in and around London. It was a place where it was possible to take refuge from the Law, being under the direction of the Church. The Westminster sanctuary was among the last to be closed down in the seventeenth century.

Diagonally opposite the Abbey is the **Methodist Central Hall** which was built between 1905 and 1911 in the Renaissance style of architecture. Between the Abbey and the Hall is the Queen Elizabeth II Conference Centre. **Westminster Abbey**, more correctly the Collegiate Church of St Peter at Westminster, stands on Thorney Eyot (Island) at the mouth of the River Tyburn. In 154 AD an earthquake destroyed the Roman temple dedicated to Apollo that stood here, and which much later was converted into a Christian Church. Over the ensuing years the building has been rebuilt several times. Today's splendid church is an example of Gothic (Medieval) architecture. It is here that royal coronations (crownings) have taken place since the time of Edward the Confessor in the eleventh century.

Standing to the side of the Abbey is the parish church of **St Margaret, Westminster**. This is the oldest church in Westminster, with the exception of the Abbey itself. It owes its origin to the saintly Confessor who built it specifically for the people of the City. Prior to having their own church, the people worshipped in the north aisle of the Abbey. There are records that tell of the constant bickering between parishioners and the monks that led to the people having a separate building for their use only.

Today, the church is under the direction of the Abbey and peace has been restored between the two factions. The present building dates from the early sixteenth century and, since 1614, has been the appointed church for members of the House of Commons. Its beautiful east window was the gift of Ferdinand and Isabella of Spain to

Henry VII on the occasion of their daughter's betrothal to Prince Arthur, the eldest son of the King of England. After passing through many hands and families, in 1758 it was bought on behalf of the Government of the time and placed in the church.

The bus now passes the former Middlesex Guildhall, now a Court of Appeal, on the left-hand side, and enters Parliament Square. Here stand statues commemorating great statesmen.

Parliament Square: Key to map

1 **St Margaret's church** A typical parish church of the early 16th century with a wide nave and side aisles. The original church was built during the reign of Edward the Confessor. It replaced the use of a side aisle in the Abbey church next door by the people of Westminster.

2 **Westminster Abbey** Until the Dissolution of the Monasteries in the sixteenth century, a Benedictine Monastery. After which, for a short time, it gained cathedral status, but later reverted to being the Collegiate Church of Saint Peter at Westminster. It is a "Royal Peculiar" answering directly to the Monarch and owing no allegiance to to either the Bishop of London or the Archbishop of Canterbury. Only the Queen walks behind the Dean of Westminster in the Abbey processions.

3 **Middlesex Guildhall** Built between 1906 and 1913 to the designs of J.S. Gibson & Partners, the Guildhall stands on the site of the detached bell tower (campanile) of the Abbey. It once served as the administrative headquarters for the former County of Middlesex.

4 **Government offices** The beginnings of the Governmental offices of Whitehall are first seen on this side of the square.

5 **Houses of Parliament** Officially The Royal Palace of Saint Stephen at Westminster, it is more commonly known as the Houses of Parliament. It is the meeting house of the Upper (Lords) House, and the Lower (Commons). The present building dates to the nineteenth century and was designed by Sir Charles Barry after a disastrous fire in 1834.

6 **Westminster Hall** One of the few medieval buildings left in Westminster, it was built in 1097 by Rufus as an extension to the Palace of Westminster built by Edward the Confessor. Its fine oak hammerbeam roof dates from the fourteenth century.

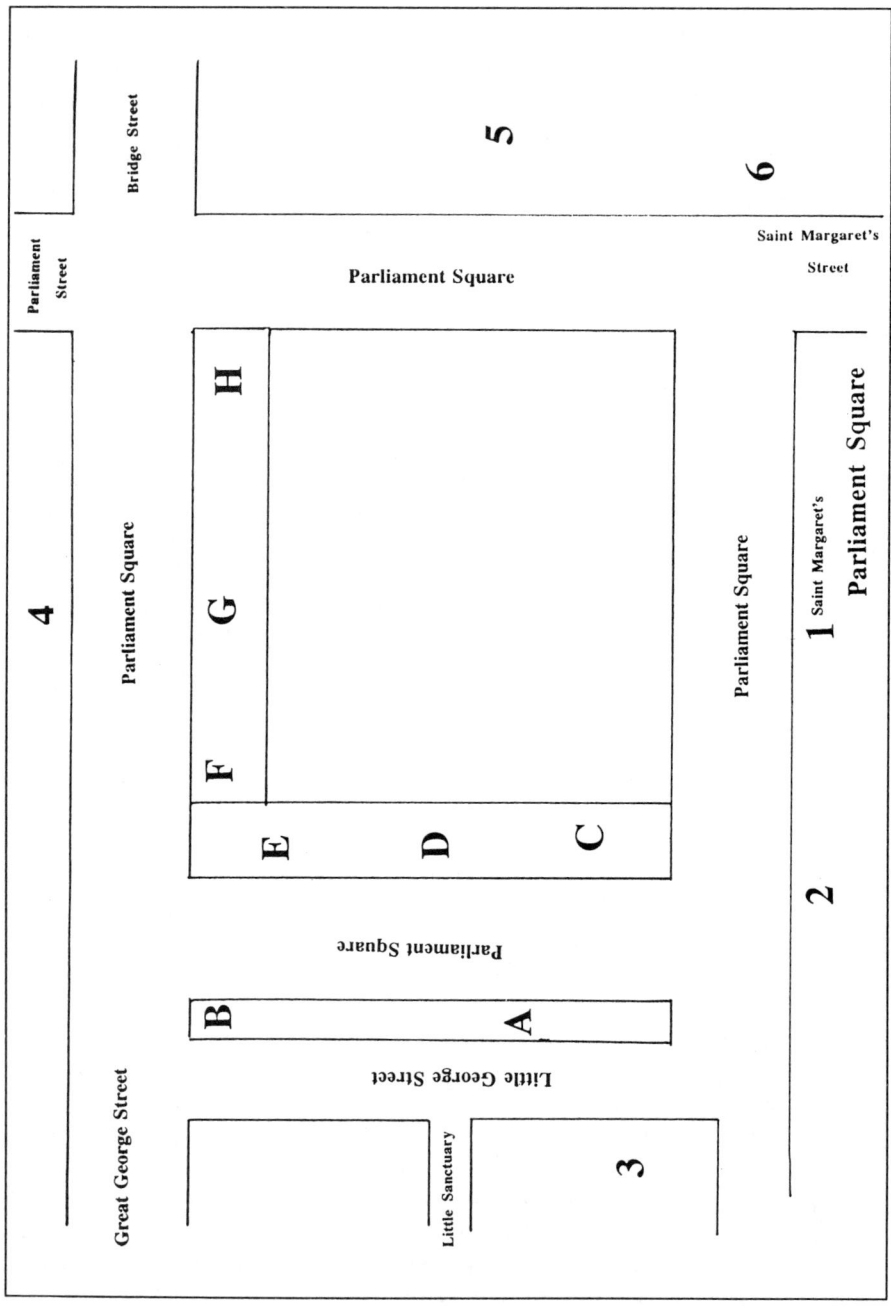

Bus Route 11: Victoria to Liverpool Street Station

A   **Abraham Lincoln** The sixteenth President of the United States of America's statue is a copy of the statue that stands in Gordon Park, Chicago. The President stands in front of a chair that is embossed with eagles, and the base has thirty-two stars around it.

B   **George Canning** A distinguished member of Parliament and well-known for his oratory. His wit and ability to disguise messages in doggerel form made him famous to some and infamous to others. One of his more famous lines were addressed to the Ambassador at The Hague: *" In matters of commerce the fault of the Dutch, Is offering too little and asking too much, The French are with equal advantage content, So we clap on Dutch bottomd just twenty percent"*

C   **Sir Robert Peel** English statesman, Prime Minister, and founder of the Metropolitan Police Force, known after him as "Peelers" or "Bobbies". He introduced a series of measures to increase financial stability, including the Bank Charter Act of 1844 and a revised income tax in 1842.

D   **Lord Beaconsfield** Born Benjamin Disraeli, he became a statesman, Prime Minister and author whose parliamentary efforts were directed to social reform and the promotion of the British Empire.

E   **Lord Derby** Three times Prime Minister in the nineteenth century, Edward Stanley was a staunch supporter of the Reform Bill and the emancipation of slaves. Note the plaques around the base that include the House of Commons, in Saint Stephen Hall before the fire of 1834.

F   **Lord Palmerston** Henry Temple, 3rd Viscount Palmerston, "personified Victorian self-confidence at its peak". His ambition to lead a nation rather than a party was realised by sheer hard work. He was twice Prime Minister and popular with everybody except the Queen – Victoria. He lies buried in the north transept of Westminster Abbey.

G   **Field Marshall Smuts** Afrikaner soldier and statesman who fought against the British in the South African War 1899-1902. He joined with Britain in the First World War and became a member of the Imperial War Cabinet in 1917. His efforts for world peace included helping with the founding of the League of Nations in 1919, and the United Nations in 1946.

H   **Sir Winston Churchill** Winston Leonard Spencer Churchill was Prime Minister during Britain's 'finest hour' (The Battle of Britain, 1940). He started his career as a soldier, then a journalist, and finally an outstanding Member of Parliament.

Whitehall: Richmond Terrace

Leaving the square, the bus turns left into Parliament Street which was built in the eighteenth century as a continuation of Whitehall. There are two or three houses on the right that remain from the original street. Just after the bus moves away from the bus stop is King Charles Street, at the end of which are the Clive Steps. Here are the **War Cabinet Rooms** from where Sir Winston Churchill and his staff masterminded the Second World War's operations. There are twenty-one rooms underneath Whitehall, and all the rooms have been preserved as they were fifty years ago. There is an admission charge to view the rooms.At the junction of Parliament Street and Whitehall stands **The Cenotaph**. In 1919, at the time of the great peace parade through London, Edwin Lutyens, the architect, was commissioned to design a focal point for the marching.columns. A plaster board construction was erected that so took the imagination of the British people that a Portland stone one replaced it after the parade. On the Sunday nearest to the 11th November, the date of the Armistice of the First World War, 1914-1918, the Nation remembers in silence the fallen of the two World Wars of this century.

A pair of fine modern gates, on the left, now guard the entrance to **Downing Street** where, at Number 10, lives the First Lord of the Treasury and Prime Minister of the United Kingdom. The house was the personal gift of George II to Sir Robert Walpole when he became the first Lord of the Treasury and Chancellor of the Exchequer. However, the office of Prime Minister was not officially recognised until 1905, when Campbell-Bannerman was given the title formally. Strictly speaking, the office of Prime Minister is an unpaid appointment. Downing Street takes its name from Sir George Downing, Member of Parliament for Carlisle, and later Morpeth, who acquired land here in 1690 and built a cul-de-sac.

To the right stands **The Banqueting House**, designed by Inigo Jones in the seventeenth century to replace the Palace of Whitehall that had been burnt to the ground. Horace Walpole, the fourth Earl of Orford, whose literary reputation rests firmly on his letters wrote, *"It is so complete in itself that it stands as the model of the most pure and beautiful taste."* It was the first purely Renaissance building in London when it was completed in 1622. Over the years it has been used for a variety of state and royal occasions, including on 30th January 1649 when Charles I walked through an open window on to the scaffold in Whitehall and was beheaded. His body lay in state in the Hall until its burial in the crypt of St George's Chapel, in Windsor Castle. During one night a visitor to the hall heard a voice from behind a curtain mutter, "It need never have happened." Shortly afterwards, Oliver Cromwell stepped out and left the hall. To the rear is the Ministry of Defence – the joint offices of the Royal Navy, Army and the Royal Air Force whose flags can be seen flying from the flagstaffs on the roof of the building. Immediately opposite the Banqueting House is the entrance to **Horse Guards Parade**, the largest and finest parade ground in Europe. On the Whitehall side stand the offices of the London District and Household Division of the Brigade of Guards. Mounted troopers stand guard from ten o'clock to four o'clock daily and are relieved hourly. The building was designed by William Kent and built between 1750 and 1780. Only members of the Royal Family are allowed to ride through the arch along with the Royal Escort – the Household Cavalry.

Shortly afterwards, on the left, stands the former **Admiralty House** with its stone screen designed by Robert Adam. The House was designed by Thomas Ripley between 1722 and 1726. It was the focal point for the Royal Navy until the setting up in 1964 of the Ministry of Defence. High above the roof line is the wireless aerial – one of the first to be set up in London. Previously messages were relayed by a series of semaphore towers from the coast to the Admiralty in London.

Whitehall leads into **Trafalgar Square**, passing *en route* the 1632 equestrian statue of Charles I by Hubert le Soeur, a Huguenot whose name and the date of the casting is on the horse's left forefoot. It was originally erected in King Street, off Covent Garden, and at the time of the king's execution was bought by a Mr Rivett, a blacksmith of Holborn. He melted the statue down and made door-knockers, door stops, and book ends from it. Loyal royal-supporters were satisfied – until the Restoration of the Monarchy in 1660. Then, the crafty blacksmith went to the bottom of his garden and dug up the complete statue of Charles I, untouched. Later he sold it to the Government who erected it on its present site.

The route takes the bus around the square to Duncannon Street by the side of St Martin-in-the-Fields parish church. Alight here to explore the square.

Trafalgar Square Walkabout

St Martin-in-the-Fields Parish Church (A) was designed by James Gibbs and consecrated in 1726. The date can be seen on the portico of the church. It is the parish church of the Admiralty, from the time when Britain's Navy Office was situated in Whitehall, and of Buckingham Palace. All baptisms performed in the Royal Chapels of St James's Palace and Buckingham Palace are entered in the church's registers. This is the only church in London to possess a Royal Pew with its own private entrance and staircase in the north-east corner of the church. After leaving the church, turn right and walk along to the statue of **Nurse Cavell (1)**. Edith Cavell was shot by the Germans for aiding the escape of Allied soldiers from Belgium during the First World War, 1914-1918. Across Charing Cross Road is the National Portrait Gallery, behind which stands a statue of **Sir Henry Irving (2)**, a nineteenth century actor-manager who was the first actor to be knighted for his services to the English theatre.

Trafalgar Square, towards St Martin's

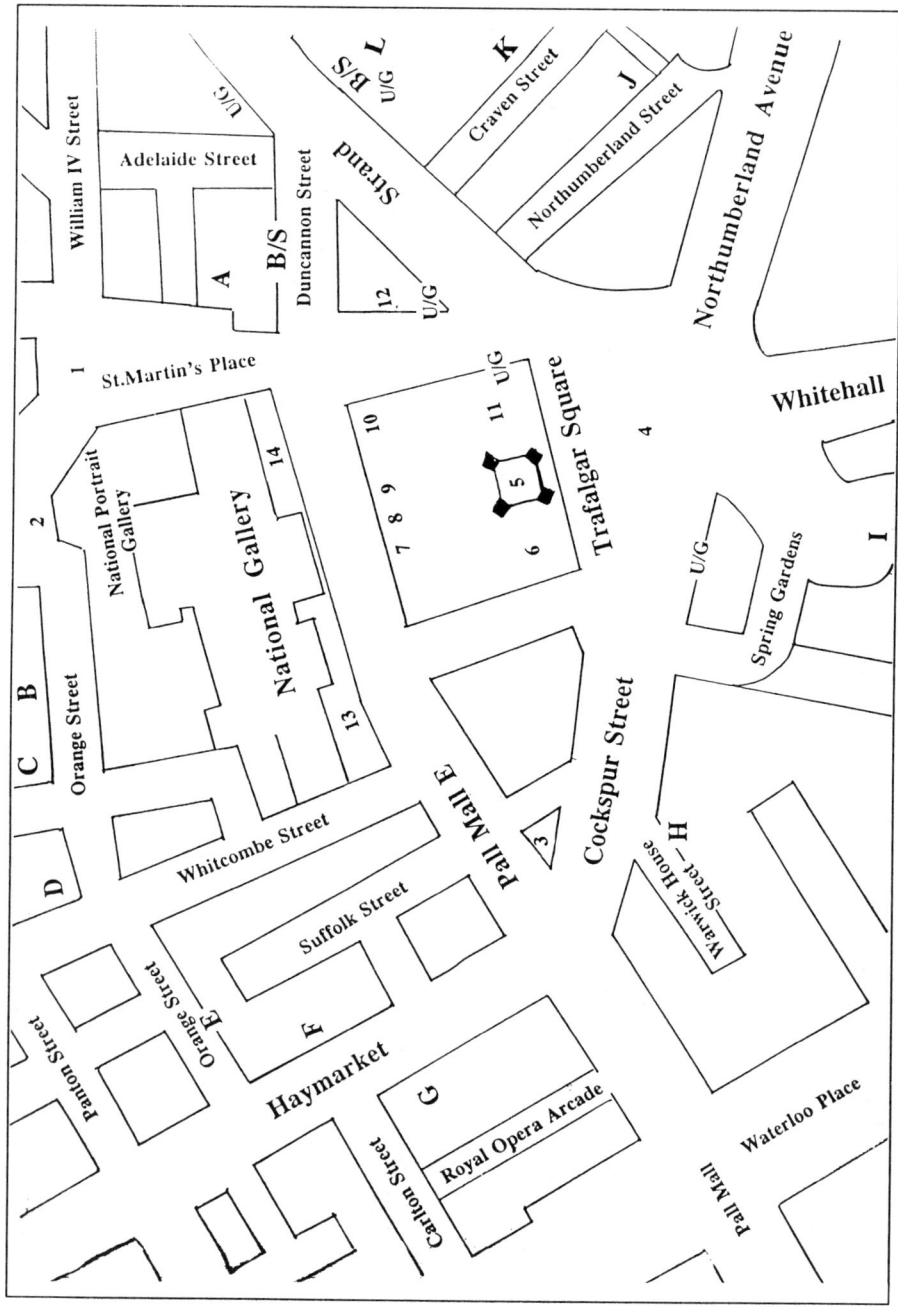

Trafalgar Square: key to map

Statues:

1. Nurse Cavell
2. Henry Irving
3. George III
4. Charles I
5. Nelson (top of column)
6. General Sir Charles James Napier
7. Admiral Lord Cunningham
8. Admiral Earl Beatty
9. Admiral Lord Jellicoe
10. George IV
11. Sir Henry Havelock
12. Bartolomeu Diaz
13. James II
14. George Washington

Buildings

A. St Martin-in-the-Fields parish church
B. Orange Street Congregational Church
C. Westminster Central Reference Library
D. Hand and Racquet Public House
E. Royal Tennis Court plaque
F. Theatre Royal
G. Her Majesty's Theatre
H. Two Chairmen Public House
I. Admiralty Arch
J. Sherlock Holmes Public House
K. Benjamin Franklin's House
L. Charing Cross Stations

In Orange Street can be seen the **Orange Street Congregational Church (B)** which stands on part of the site of a Huguenot chapel established here in 1693. During the eighteenth century it became a Church of England Chapel under the care of The Rev'd. Augustus Toplady who wrote the hymn "Rock of Ages". It is said that he was inspired to write the words while sheltering under some rocks in the Cheddar Gorge during a thunderstorm. The present building was erected in 1929. Near to the chapel, in St Martin's Street, is the **Central Reference Library (C)**. Part of the Library service of the Westminster City Council, it houses one of the finest collections of reference books outside the national collection at the British Museum. It is built on the site of the house of Sir Isaac Newton, the discoverer of the earth's gravity. On the next street corner is the **Hand and Racquet Public House (D)** that calls to mind the Royal Tennis Courts that used to be here. These are recalled on the **plaque (E)** further along the street. At the end of Orange Street is the Haymarket. Here are two of London's famous theatres. On the left is the **Theatre Royal (F)** which was designed by John Nash, the Prince Regent's (later George IV) favourite architect. On the opposite side of the roadway is **Her Majesty's Theatre (G)**. The latter was rebuilt in 1869 after a disastrous fire wrecked the entire theatre. Walk down the Haymarket, cross over the road, and find Warwick House Street. The House has long since disappeared but there is an interesting little public house here – the **Two Chairmen (H)**. The name is a reminder of a form of transport in the eighteenth century – the sedan chair. Returning once more to Cockspur Street, turn right and follow the pavement round until the **Admiralty Arch (I)** is reached. The arch was part of the redevelopment of The Mall as a memorial to Queen Victoria in the early part of this century. It was the work of the architect Sir Aston Webb. Cross over the end of Whitehall and walk down Northumberland Avenue to the **Sherlock Holmes Public House (J)**. In the upper restaurant there is a reconstruction of the front room of 221B Baker Street, and on the walls of the ground floor memorabilia of Sherlock Holmes and his creator, Sir Arthur Conan Doyle. To the right-hand side of the public house is a short passageway that leads into Craven Street. Number 36 was the home of the American scientist and statesman, **Benjamin Franklin (K)**. When, in 1757, he came to England as Agent to the General Assembly of Pennsylania he wrote to his wife, "The whole town is one great smoakly (sic) house and every street a chimney..." It is hoped to restore the house as a museum and a meeting place. At the end of the street is the Strand, **Charing Cross Stations (L),** and in Duncannon Street, the bus stop that will take you on the next part of your journey.

Return to the bus to continue the journey when the bus passes along the Strand. Immediately ahead is Charing Cross (British Rail) Station which was designed by John Hawkshaw, consulting engineer to the South Eastern Railway, and opened in 1864. The site was previously occupied by the Hungerford Market. In the station's forecourt stands E.M. Barry's replica of an Eleanor Cross. The original cross stood where the statue of Charles I can now be seen at the head of Whitehall. It was the last of twelve crosses erected in 1291 to commemorate where the body of Edward I's first wife, Eleanor of Castile, rested on its way to burial in Westminster Abbey. It was from this station that the legendary Sherlock Holmes, with Doctor Watson, left for Switzerland in pursuit of Doctor Moriarty.

At the end of this first portion of the Strand, the bus turns into the Aldwych, and by alighting at the bus stop by the Strand Theatre, it is convenient to explore the area around Covent Garden.

Covent Garden & Aldwych: key to map

Note that this map is used for the following *two* 'walkabouts'.

- *A*   Bush House
- *B*   Australia House
- *C*   St Clement Danes
- *D*   "Roman" Bath
- *E*   St Mary Le Strand
- *F*   King's College
- *G*   Somerset House
- *H*   Courtauld Galleries
- *I*   Savoy Chapel

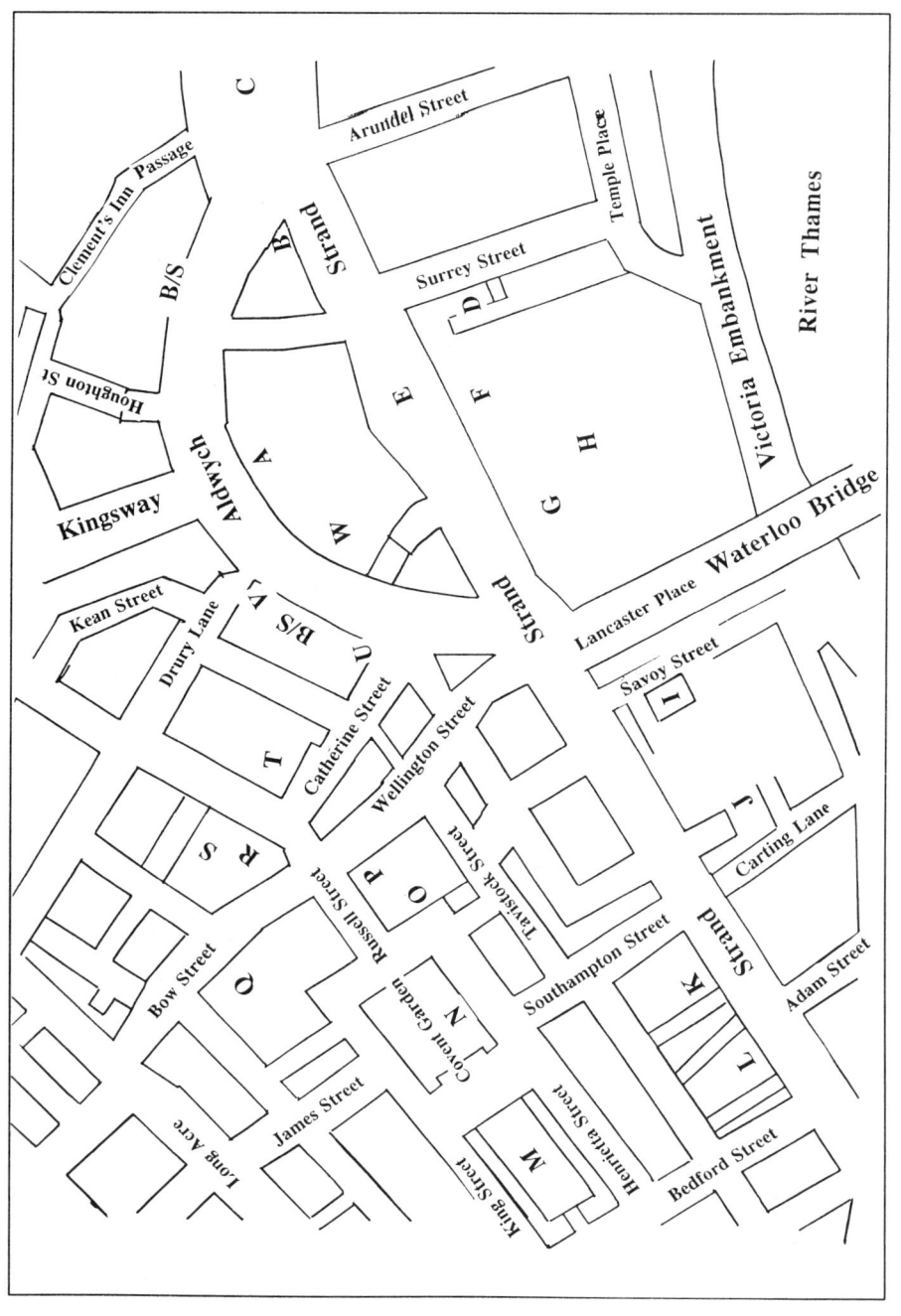

Bus Route 11: Victoria to Liverpool Street Station

J Savoy Hotel
K Adelphi Theatre
L Vaudeville Theatre
M St Paul's Church
N Covent Garden Market
O London Transport Museum
P Theatre Museum
Q Royal Opera house
R Fortune Theatre
S Scottish Church
T Theatre Royal
U Strand Theatre
V Aldwych Theatre
W India House

Covent Garden Walkabout

Near Southampton Street, on the north side of the Strand, is the **Vaudeville Theatre (K)** built in 1870 by C.J. Phipps, with the **Adelphi (L)** rebuilt in 1901-1902 a few steps away. To reach Covent Garden, walk along the Strand to Bedford Street and then past Henrietta Street to Inigo Place. This is the entrance to the churchyard of **St Paul's Church, Covent Garden (M)**. The church was consecrated in 1638 and was designed by Inigo Jones. "It was the first new Anglican church to be built in London since the Reformation of the sixteenth century." Today, in addition to being the parish church for Covent Garden, it is also the parish church of the Actors' Church Union. Many famous actors and actresses are buried here, including in the south wall of the church the ashes of Ellen Terry. Much of the wall space in the church is covered with wooden commemorative plaques of persons of the theatrical world. Leave the churchyard by way of one of the side doorways either into King Street or Henrietta Street and walk along to **Covent Garden (N)**.

Among the earliest of the squares that still grace certain areas of London, the Covent Garden piazza was designed by Inigo Jones as part of the Duke of Bedford's estate north of the Strand in the seventeenth century. Originally it was part of the Con(v)ent Garden of Westminster Abbey. The Benedictine monks grew vegetables and fruit here for their own consumption. Any surplus was sold and the money used for the upkeep of the abbey buildings. After the dissolution of the abbey in the late sixteenth century the land was acquired by the Crown and it was then given to John Russell, 1st Earl of Bedford. Later in the seventeenth century a market came into being and served London until 1974 when it was moved to Nine Elms, Vauxhall, on the south side of the river. The buildings, by Charles Fowler, the architect, were then restored and have become a very popular tourist attraction. In the south-east corner of the piazza is the **London Transport Museum (O)**. Opened in 1980, it represents nearly two hundred years of transport in the capital. There is an admission charge.

Covent Garden: tables & chairs

A short walk away, on the corner of Russell Street, is the **Theatre Museum (P)** where there is an extensive collection of material relating to all aspects of the performing arts. The collection is not limited to the theatres of London, but includes items from the Palace Theatre, Glasgow and other parts of the United Kingdom. There is an admission charge. Walk up Bow Street to find the **Royal Opera House (Q)** which was first built in 1732 as the Covent Garden Theatre. The present (third) building was designed by E.M. Barry, son of Sir Charles Barry the architect of the Houses of Parliament at Westminster. It was opened in 1858 and today is the home of one of the finest opera companies in the world. Return to Russell Street to see the **Fortune Theatre (R)** which was founded in 1924 by Laurence Cowen and mainly used during its infancy for amateur productions. The theatre thrives today with modern professional plays. The building was designed by Ernest Schaufelberg who was also the sculptor of the bronze figure of "The Nude" on the facade. To the left of the building is a doorway that leads into the **Crown Court Church (S)**. Taking its name from the Crown Tavern, the Court today is a pedestrian way which leads to Broad Court and Bow Street

Magistrates' Court. The church, built in 1909 to the design of Balfour and Turner, in a neo-Elizabethan style, houses the National Scottish Church. The congregation is made up of the Scottish community that is scattered all over London, drawing members to the church from both London and the Home Counties (Surrey, Kent, Essex, Hertfordshire, and the former County of Middlesex).

On the corner of Catherine Street stands the **Theatre Royal, Drury Lane (T).** The first theatre was built in 1663 for Thomas Killigrew and the King's Company. Nell Gwynne made her debut here in 1665 in a play by Dryden called "Indian Queen". The present 'new' theatre was opened in 1812, modelled on the great theatre of Bordeaux, to the designs of Benjamin Wyatt, The colonnade was added in 1831. The pillars came from John Nash's Quadrant in Regent Street. At the further end of the lane from the theatre is the Aldwych where there are two more theatres – the **Strand (U)** and the **Aldwych (V).** Opposite the theatres is **India House (W)**, designed by Sir Herbert Baker and A.T. Scott and built between 1928 and 1930 as Offices for the High Commissioners of India. The interiors are the work of Indian artists.

The Aldwych Walkabout

On returning to the Strand Theatre, a walk around Aldwych will reveal much of interest to the visitor, and Londoner, alike. The walk begins from **Bush House (A)** at the southern end of Kingsway which houses the BBC's External Radio Services. While it is not open to the public to visit, its services will be well-known to many visitors to London. Over the main entrance to the building there are two four metre (12ft) male figures, "Youth" by Malvina Hoffman (1928), that represent England and America. Underneath are the words, "To the friendship of the English speaking peoples." Leaving Bush House on the right, walk round to **Australia House (B)** and admire the statuary around and above the main entrance. Across the roadway is the church of **Saint Clement Danes (C),** the Central Church of the Royal Air Force. Inside can be seen, on the floor of the nave, the crests of the various squadrons of the RAF, and in the show cases around the church are listed the airmen who died in the Second World War. From the church, leading towards the River Thames, is Surrey Street.

Halfway down on the right-hand side there is an entrance under the building. Walk down the passage to the steps at the end and the **"Roman" Bath (D)** is nearby. To view the bath, press the light button at the side of the window. Authorities differ as to what it exactly was built for, but it is hardly conceivable that it was used in Roman days to bathe in – it would have been halfway up the river bank, and in the open! Return to the Strand. Shortly, on the right, standing on its own island in the middle of the roadway, is the parish church of **St Mary Le Strand (E).** Considered by many to be the finest Baroque church in London, if not in England itself, it has stood here from the early eighteenth century, and like St Martin-in-the-Fields is the work of James Gibbs, the Scottish Catholic architect. The lower walling is solid, an attempt to keep out the noise of the passing traffic. Its ceiling, by plasterers Chrysostem and John Wilkins, is worthy to be rated alongside their contemporary Italian counterparts. Opposite the church is **King's College, London (F),** one of the many colleges of the University of London. Next to the college is **Somerset House (G)**, the home of the Courtauld Institute of Art's fine collection of paintings. Continue to walk along the Strand, cross over the roadway (Lancaster Place) and shortly on the left is Savoy Hill and the **Savoy Chapel (I)**. Originally part of the Royal Palace of the Savoy, today it is the Chapel of the Royal Victorian Order. The Order was founded on 21st April 1896 and is entirely the gift of the sovereign, "for service rendered to the Crown". Return once again to the Strand and turn left. Either side of an entrance to a passageway, two ceramic shields with inscriptions can be seen. One says, "This way was called Fountain Court until 1883 from the Fountain Tavern which stood on this site." The other notes, "In this court in the 18th century stood the Fountain Tavern where the political opponents of Sir Robert Walpole using the title of the Fountain Club also the Coal Hole the meeting place of the Wolfe Club of which about 1826 Edmund Kean was a leading member." The **Savoy Hotel (J)** was designed by T. Colcutt and built in 1889 on part of the site of the Royal Palace of the Savoy. There were extensive additions to the hotel in the earlier part of this century. The roadway leading to the main entrance is the only place where vehicles drive on the right-hand side.

Fountain Court ceramic

Return to the bus-stop to continue the journey round the Aldwych when it returns to another portion of the Strand. On the right is the Central Church of the Royal Air Force – St Clement Danes. This was rebuilt in the late seventeenth century by Sir Christopher Wren, and its tower and spire added later by James Gibbs. It is one of two churches associated with the nursery rhyme "Oranges and Lemons", the other church being St Clement Eastcheap in the City of London where citrus fruits were unloaded at a wharf in the parish. Every year, towards the end of March, children from St Clement Danes Church of England Primary School, in Drury Lane, attend a service at which they are given an orange and lemon. So a tradition survives!

Opposite the church, on the left, are the **Royal Courts of Justice** (the Law Courts) opened by Queen Victoria on 4th December 1882. They replace the old superior courts of Westminster and are made up of the Court of Appeal, the High Court, and the Crown Court. The High Court consists of three Divisions. The Queen's Bench Division deals with civil actions involving contract or tort. Chancery Division deals with the administration of estates, including those of deceased persons, partnerships and mortgages, contractual rights, execution of trusts and settlements. The Family Division was once known as the Wills, Wives and Wrecks Division when it was part of the Probate, Divorce and Admiralty Division. In 1969 the Divorce Division was changed to the Family Division.

On the right can be seen The Wig and Pen restaurant, formerly a wining and dining club; it is now open to members of the general public. As a club it was intended for "men of Law and Writers" and was housed here in two seventeenth century houses.

In the centre of the roadway stands a column surmounted by a dragon (the symbol of the City of London). Designed by Sir Horace Jones, the City Architect, with panels by Sir Edgar Boehm, it commemorates the site of the Temple Bar. It marks the boundary of the City of London and the end of the jurisdiction of the Lord Mayor, Sheriffs and Common Council of the City. Until its removal in 1870, the gatehouse designed by Christopher Wren that stood here, hindered the flow of traffic in and out of the City. At the present time the structure is mouldering away at Theobalds Park in Hertfordshire. There are plans to rebuild it, possibly by the side of St Paul's Cathedral when the area to the north of the cathedral is redeveloped.

After Temple Bar, Fleet Street is entered. Once the home of the national newspapers, and with offices of many of the regional and international papers as well, today the printing presses have moved out to Docklands and the South Bank. Immediately on the right can be seen **Prince Henry's Room**, a seventeenth century meeting place for the Council of the Principality of Wales. Today it houses a collection of memorabilia of Samuel Pepys whose diary so vividly tells of the Great Plague of 1665 and the Great Fire of 1666. Note the fleur-de-lis and the motto "Ich Dien" (I Serve) on the outside of the building. It is possible to visit the room Mondays to Fridays from 11am to 2pm and to inspect the exhibits placed there by the Samuel Pepys Club of London.

St Dunstan-in-the-West parish church was rebuilt in 1831 by John Shaw and replaces a church that was pulled down in a roadway widening scheme at that time. Today the church is the centre for the Church of England's Council on Foreign Affairs. In addition to the Anglican services, the building is used by seven Orthodox Churches for their services. To the right of the tower is a seventeenth century clock with two ancient warriors whose clubs strike out the hours.

A glimpse of the tower and steeple of the parish church of **St Bride, Fleet Street** may be seen on the right-hand side just before the traffic lights at Ludgate Circus. Among the famous and the infamous buried in the former south churchyard are Richard Lovelace, poet and cavalier, who wrote one of the most famous, and often quoted lines in English poetry: "Stone walls do not a prison make". A near "neighbour" is Mary Frith, more popularly known as "Moll Cut-purse", a notorious pickpocket, fortune-teller, forger and highway robber.

Ludgate Circus passes over the River Fleet, long since buried underground, but in earlier times navigable a mile or two upstream from Blackfriars where it joins the River Thames. From the Circus the roadway leads up Ludgate Hill to St Paul's Cathedral, passing on its way the parish church of **St Martin-within-Ludgate**, the gate being one of the eight medieval entrances to the City of London. The church is said to have been founded in the seventh century by Cadwalla. The present building was built by Sir Christopher Wren after the Great Fire of 1666.

Ahead can be seen **St Paul's Cathedral** in all its glory. Rebuilt after the Great Fire by Sir Christopher Wren, it is the third cathedral to be built on this site and is well worth breaking the journey to visit. In front of the cathedral stands the replica statue of Queen Anne by Francis Bird. The original sculpture is now in East Sussex. It can be seen from the road in the grounds of a convent at Holmhurst St Mary. The figures around the plinth of the statue represent Britannia, Ireland, France and America. Strangely, England had not owned any land in France for a number of years when Anne was Queen!

St Paul's: south east view

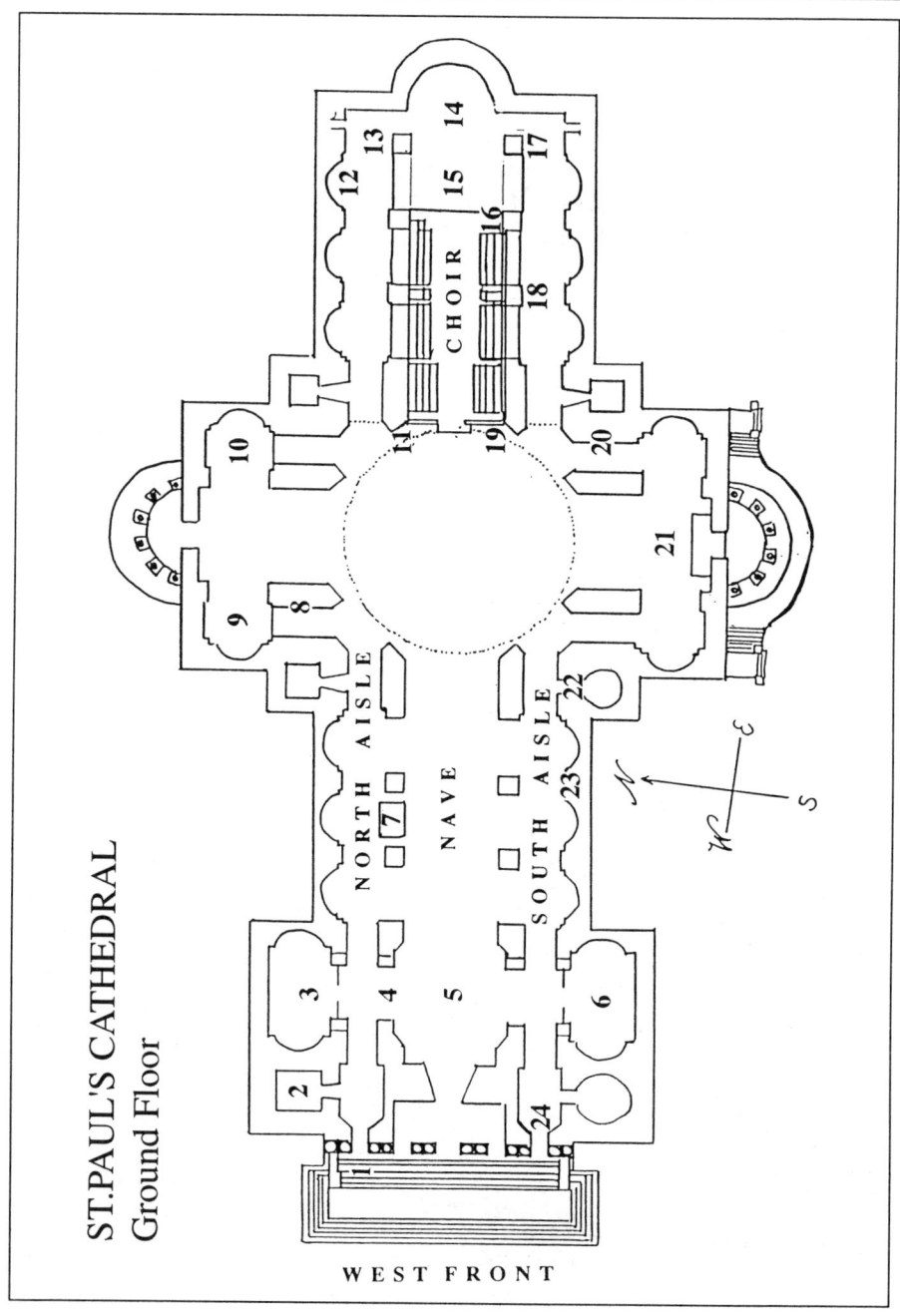

St Paul's Cathedral Trail

The following trail of the cathedral is offered for those with but a short time to spare.

1. North West door
To enter the cathedral climb the steps on the left (north west) side of the building. At the foot of the steps can be seen the inscription conglomerating the Diamond Jubilee of Queen Victoria in 1897.

2. All Souls' Chapel
Immediately on the left after entering the building is the Chapel of All Souls, or the Kitchener Memorial Chapel. Built originally as the base of the bell tower it was transformed into a chapel in the 1920s. Inscribed on the west wall is a tablet recording the creation of the chapel as a memorial to Lord Kitchener, who was drowned when *HMS Hampshire* was sunk off the coast of Orkney lsland in 1916. The candlesticks and altar cross are made from the silver sporting trophies won by men killed in the First World War.

3. St Dunstan's Chapel
This chapel was originally designed to provide a place where the clergy and others say could attend the early morning service. Hence it is shown on early plans as the Morning Chapel. It was renamed St Dunstan's in 1909, and today is set aside for private prayer. Visitors are asked to respect this and not to enter.

4. Ticket desk
A charge is made towards the upkeep of the building. This covers visits to the ground floor and the crypt of the cathedral. A further charge is made for those wishing to ascend to the Whispering Gallery and the outside gallery around the foot of the dome

5. Nave
From here can be seen the great length of the cathedral with the High Altar in the distance. Before moving on, look down and read the inscription on the floor.

6. Order of St Michael & St George Chapel
This is the Chapel of the Order of St Michael and St George which was instituted in 1818 and was intended as an honour for military and naval officers who rendered distinguished service in Britain's Mediterranean colonies and protectorates. In 1869 is was extended to cover all other parts

of the, then, British Empire. It ranks fifth in the seven British Orders of Knighthood.

7. Duke of Wellington's monument
Half way down the nave, on the left-hand side, is the monumental memorial to the first Duke of Wellington, Arthur Wellesley, the victor of the Battle of Waterloo in 1815. The monument, which took twenty years to complete, was the work of Alfred Stevens and is considered to be one of the most celebrated English works of art of the nineteenth century. His tomb is to be found in the crypt of the cathedral.

8. Mother and Child
This terracotta sculpture is the work of Josephina de Vasconfellos and was given to the Dean and Chapter in 1957. Look for her "signature" – a mouse in the lower folds of her dress.

9. Font
This font, from which the Sacrament of Baptism is administered was the work of Francis Bird and is made of Carrara marble from Italy. It cost £350 and was installed in the cathedral in 1727. When in use, a small portion of the top is removed from the north side. Look for the two small brass holes into which "keys" are inserted to lift out the door. Peter Burman in his "St Paul's Cathedral" in the New Bell's Cathedral Series describes the font as being "rather like a gigantic salt cellar".

10. Middlesex Regiment Chapel
In the opposite corner of the north transept from the font is the Middlesex Regiment's Chapel whose regimental colours hang from the wall.

11. Lectern
Designed in the form of an eagle, the lectern is of gilt metal, and was made in 1720 by Jacob Sutton at a cost of £241. Eagles are said to be able to fly highest in the sky, so taking the petitions of the people heavenwards; since they can also fly the longest distances without rest, they also symbolically take the good news of the Gospel to the furthest lands of the earth. In Medieval days the open beak was often used to receive monetary offerings. The round orb at its feet could then be unscrewed to redeem the money.

12. Mother & Child by Henry Moore
The sculptor himself choose the position of this Travertine stone figure of the Virgin and Child. It was placed here in 1983 to be a free-standing effigy that can be admired from all angles.

13. Chapel of the Modern Martyrs
Here are commemorated Anglican martyrs who are known from 1850. It was consecrated in 1962 and has an altar of wood painted to look like

marble. The crucifix was part of the Bodley and Garner high altar reredos that was severely damaged in the last War and not replaced.

14. American Memorial Chapel
Dedicated in November 1918 by the then Bishop of London, William Wand, to the memory of the 28,000 servicemen who died while based in the United Kingdom during World War Two. The significant dates on the altar rail are:- 607, First Christian church on the site; 1300, Consecration of Old St Paul's; 1607, First English settlement at Jameston, Virginia; 1666, Destruction of Old St Paul's by fire; 1710, Consecration of present St Paul's; 1778, Declaration of American Independence. Inscriptions in the chapel include, in Hebrew, the first commandment "Thou shalt have none other Gods but me" (in memory of the Jewish dead) and on the floor: "To the American Dead of the second world war from the people of Britain".

15. High Altar & Baldaccino
Erected in 1958 "by the people of Britain" as a memorial to the 335,454 men and women of the Commonwealth Overseas who died in the two world wars of this century. It is made of pure Sicilian marble, the top of which weighs 4.5725 tonnes (4.5 tons).

16. "Cathedra" – bishop's throne
This is traditionally the seat on which the bishop sat and taught his clergy. today it is used by the bishop when he attends services in which he is to play a part. At other times he has a seat among the choir stalls.

17. Lady chapel
The statue of the Virgin Mary and the Child Jesus is another piece of the former Victorian reredos of the high altar. Like the other two chapels at the east end of the cathedral this one is of a recent, 1950s, date. The frame around this statue is part of Wren's great organ screen that was dismantled in 1858. The carved wooden altar table was the original high altar designed by Wren and carved by William Samwell. The candlesticks and crucifix were presented by the President of the Germany Republic as a gift from the German people.

18. Effigy of John Donne
The only surviving complete monument from Old Paul's is the one of John Donne, Dean of St Paul's from 1621 to 1631, who was also well-known for his poetry and wit. The statue is based on a painting that was commissioned by Dr. Fox, a friend of the Dean and which, after his death, was used as a study for the stone effigy. Ironically, the painting perished in a house fire, and the effigy survived the Great Fire of London of 1666.

19. Pulpit
Designed by the late Lord Mottistone who, from 1957 to 1963, was the

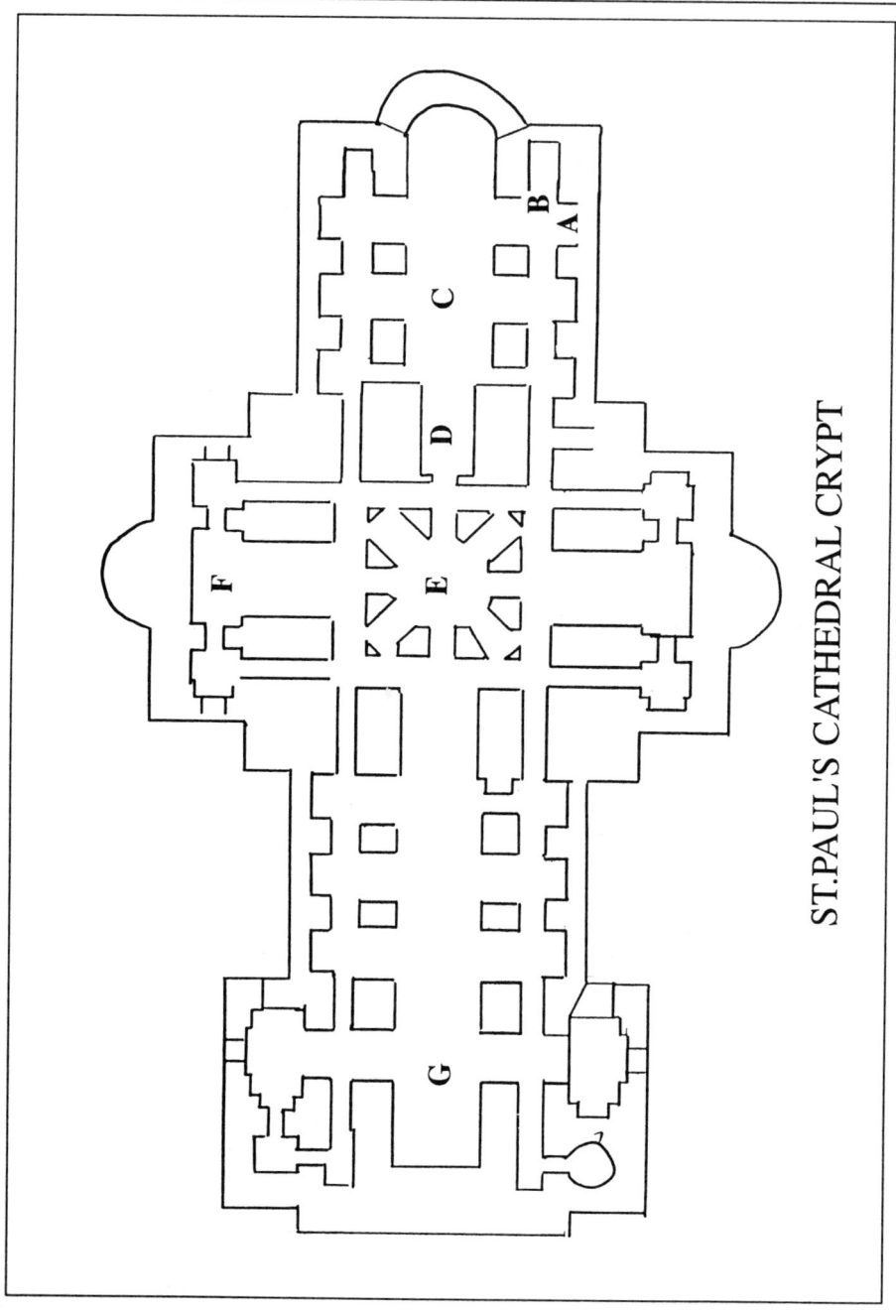

ST.PAUL'S CATHEDRAL CRYPT

Surveyor of the fabric of the cathedral. It was erected by H.H. Martyn and Co., Ltd. The limewood carvings were the work of E.J. and A.T. Bradford, Ltd.. The figure of Christ is by Edwin Russell, the sculptor, and this replaces the one erected in 1883 as a memorial to Captain Robert Fitzgerald of the Indian Army. He was taken ill on the return journey to England and died, some say, of sunstroke!

20. Entrance to the Crypt

21. Part of the former Organ screen
When Wren's great organ screen was dismantled in 1858, part of it was used here to form a small balcony with additional seating.

22. Stairs to the Dome
Here for a further small charge it is possible to climb the stairs to the Whispering Gallery, and then go on to the stone Gallery at the base of the Dome. For the more energetic, there is a further flight of stairs that leads to the gallery that surrounds the top of the dome. From here, on a clear, day the vista is 'out of this world".

23. Holman Hunt's "Light of the World"
Hunt's "Sermon in a frame" was presented to the Dean and Chapter of the cathedral by the Rt. Hon Charles Booth, social reformer and pioneer of old age pensions. It shows Christ knocking on the door on which there is no handle. The door represents man's heart that can only be opened to Christ if he is let in. This painting is a larger copy of the original that is in the chapel of Keble College, Oxford. The two paintings are not identical and a comparison between them would reveal many changes that Holman Hunt made in the later picture.

24. Exit door if not visiting the crypt.

Key to the crypt

A. Sir Christopher Wren
Although it was the intention of the Dean and Chapter of the cathedral not to allow anyone to be buried within the walls of the building they relented and permitted him to be "laid to rest" in a far corner of the crypt. The black marble stone simply records: "Here lieth Sir Christopher Wren Kt the Builder of this Cathedral Church of ST PAUL, &c., who Dyed in the Year of our Lord MDCCXXIII, and of his Age XCI." Above is the inscription that was first placed in the North Transept of the cathedral in the last century and later removed to the crypt. It ends with the immortal words 'Lectore, si monementul requiris, circumspice" (Reader, if you seek a memorial: look around you).

B. Tomb of Holman Hunt
English painter and a member of the Pre-Raphaelite Brotherhood that also included Dante Gabriel Rossetti and Sir John Millais (who is also buried near to Wren).

C. Chapel of the Order of the British Empire
The Order was founded in 1917 to reward men and women who had given conspicuous service at home, in India and other parts of the world. It was dedicated in the presence of Her Majesty The Queen and the Duke of Edinburgh in May 1960. Lord Mottistone designed the chhapel and Brian Thomas was responsible for the stained glass and the transparencies on the screen.

D. Tomb of the Duke of Wellington
The sarcophagus in which one of England's greatest heroes lies is made of two blocks of Cornish porphyry that rest on a base of granite. It is one of the most impressive tombs in the cathedral.

E. Tomb of Horatio, Viscount Nelson
Nelson's resting place is as ornate as Wellington's is plain and is sited exactly under the centre of the dome. It was intended to house the body of Cardinal Wolsey, but when he fell from power in the sixteenth century it was 'acquired' by Henry VIII for himself. But, when he died he was buried in the Royal Vaults under St George's chapel in Windsor Castle. The pieces lay in a stone mason's yard until the death of Nelson when they were used for his burial here in the cathedral. Before moving away, look down at the mosaic flooring around the tomb. This later addition was laid circa. 1850 by women prisoners from Woking Jail, in Surrey. The crocodile commemorates the Battle of the Nile, and the frogs are reminders of battles with the French.

F. Treasury
The treasury was opened in November 1981, and houses a unique collection of ecclesiastical items. Here can be seen chalices and patens, the plates and cups, used in the celebration of the service of Holy Communion, many of which are on loan from both the City of London Churches as well as from other parts of the Diocese of London. There is also a fine collection of books and vestments of which there is no finer than the one in the centre cabinet. Made to commemorate the Silver Jubilee of Her Majesty The Queen in 1977 by Miss Beryl Dean's evening classes at the Stanhope Institute. The Jubilee Cope includes in its design St Paul's Cathedral, seventy-three churches, three Royal Peculiars as well as Westminster Abbey.

G. Book shop and exit
Here you can buy books, souvenirs and other tourist items. The way out

from the shop leads to the north side of the cathedral. It is possible to visit the shop without going through the cathedral, but not the other way round.

Opposite the cathedral is the City of London's Information Centre where information about the City can be obtained. At the east end of the cathedral is the Choir School where the choristers receive their education. It was designed by Leo de Syllas of the Architects Co-Partnership and replaces the Victorian building in Carter Lane that has now been taken over by the Youth Hostel Association (YHA). The tower and spire are all that remains of the former parish church of St Augustine, Watling Street. This was rebuilt by Wren after the Great Fire, but bombed then not rebuilt after the Second World War.

- end of Cathedral trail -

Just past the traffic lights, the roadway divides to the right towards the Tower of London and to the left to the Bank of England. We take the left and pass the parish church of **St Mary Aldermary**. Unlike his other City churches that he built in the classical style, this one was rebuilt by Wren in the Gothic. Recent research has revealed that much of the previous building had survived the Great Fire. When Wren was called upon to rebuild the church in the former style, he used much of what remained from the earlier church. In today's terminology, he refurbished the building rather than started from new foundations.

Queen Victoria Street, one of the new roadways of the nineteenth century, leads to the Bank (of England). On the right can be seen the foundations of the Mithraic Temple that was found during the rebuilding of the city after the last War. The Cult of Mithras spread throughout the Roman Empire. It had its origins in Persia (Iran) in the second century, and was particularly popular along the Rhine and Danube rivers. Membership included both soldiers and state officials, among whom it was considered to be socially respectable. The temples were dark and cave-like in construction, reflecting the Romans' conception of the Universe – a cosmic cave. It was an all-male cult with seven grades of initiation, each of which reflected the rise of the soul through planetary spheres. The temple's focal point was a stone carving showing Mithras slaying a bull. All the items found on the site are now on display in the Museum of London, London Wall. At the end of the street is the **Mansion House**, the home of the Lord Mayor of London during his year of office. The foundation stone was laid in 1739, but the building was not ready for occupation until 1752 when the Lord Mayor, Sir Crisp Gascoyne, was able to take up residence. It is not open to the general public.

Ahead, at the end of Threadneedle Street, is **The Bank of England**. Founded in 1694, it started its role as the Government's Banker and Debt-Manager on the 27th July that year. It still performs these functions today. The first "home" for the bank was temporary accommodation in the hall of the Worshipful Company of Mercers in Cheapside. There were seventeen clerks and two gatekeepers. It moved to the hall of the Worshipful Company of Grocers later the same year, and remained there until 1734 when it bought land on the site where it still stands today. The building now occupies 1.2 hectares (3 acres) and retains the massive outside walls of Sir John Soane's building. Between the two World Wars of this century, a further rebuilding programme was carried out by Sir Herbert Baker. Although the Bank itself is not open to the general public for visiting, there is an excellent Museum in Bartholomew Lane to the side of the building. Admission is free!

The Bank area: key to map

- *A*   Bank of England
- *B*   Museum entrance
- *C*   Royal Exchange Bldg
- *D*   Merchant Taylors' Hall
- *E*   St Peter-upon-Cornhill
- *F*   St Michael Cornhill
- *G*   St Mary Woolnoth
- *H*   St Clement Eastcheap
- *I*   The Monument
- *J*   Cannon Street Stns
- *K*   Tallow Chandlers' Hall
- *L*   St Stephen Walbrook
- *M*   Mithraic Temple
- *N*   Mansion House

Bus Route 11: Victoria to Liverpool Street Station

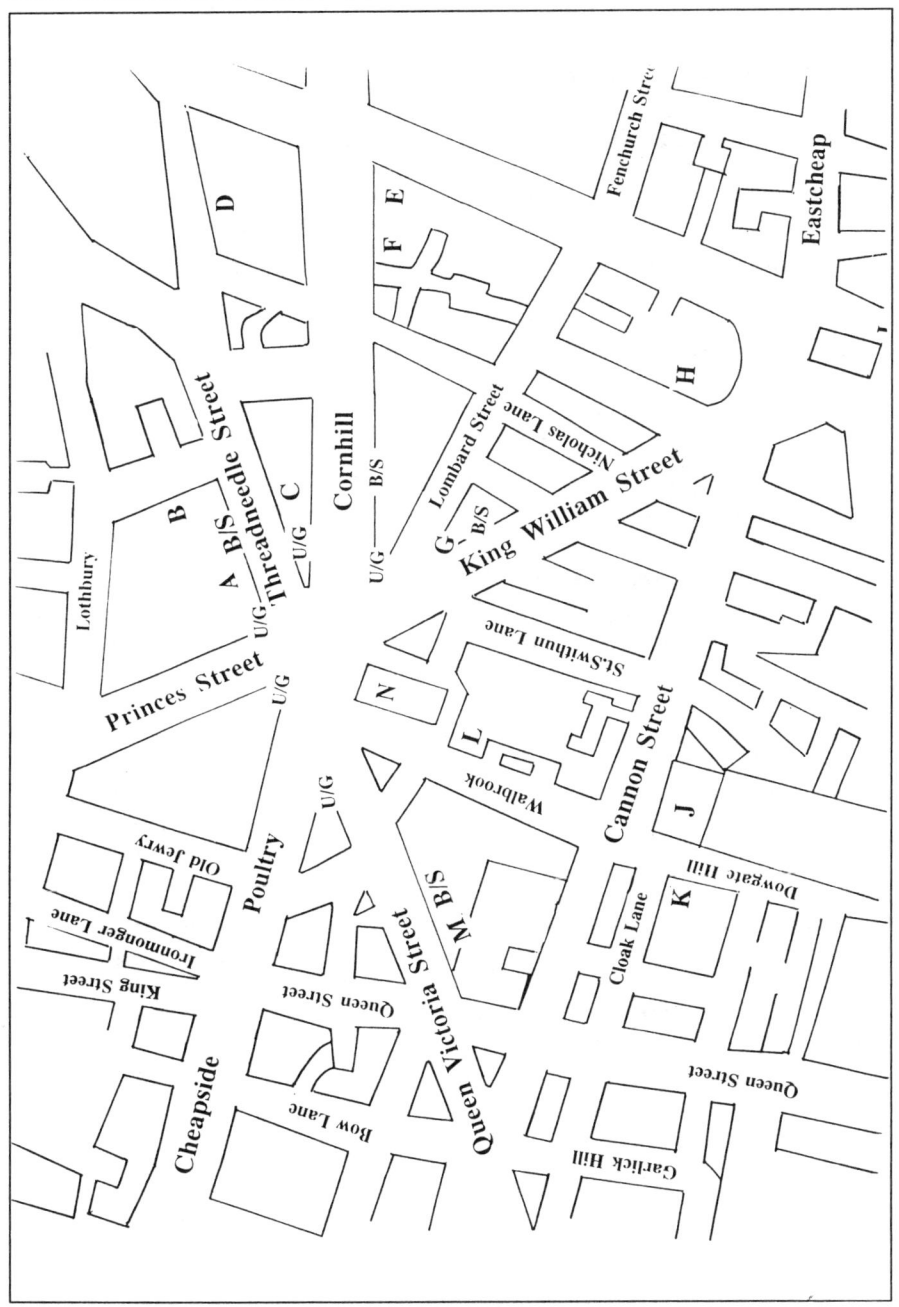

Bank

A **Bank of England** Founded in 1694, the present building was erected during the 1920s and 1930s. It was designed by Sir Herbert Baker, with the lower walls being retained from the previous building by Sir John Soane. Today the main functions of the Bank are to act as a note-issuing authority, as the government and bankers' bank, as manager of the National Debt, and as custodian of the nation's gold reserve.

B **Museum entrance** The entrance to the Bank of England Museum is in Batholomew Lane, at the side of the Bank. It traces the history of the Bank from its foundation to the high-tech world of modern banking. Admission is free, and daily except Saturday, but it is open on Lord Mayor's Show day.

C **Royal Exchange Building** Opened in 1568 as a meeting place for City merchants, today it is used by the London International Futures Exchange. Traditionally, important proclamations are declared from in front of the building. These include declarations of war and accessions to the Throne.

D **Merchant Taylors' Hall** "The Guild of Merchant Taylors of the Fraternity of St John the Baptist in the City of London", so reads the Royal Charter granted in 1503. Although not directly concerned today with the trade of tailoring, it does give awards and scholarships within the scope of its original Charter.

E **St Peter-upon-Cornhill** According to a brass inscription in the former vestry, the earliest church on this site dated from 179 AD, and was erected by King Lucius. It has a Bernard Schmitt (Father Smith) organ on whose keyboard Mendelssohn played. He left a note to say that he had played on it! The church is not normally open to visitors.

F **St Michael Cornhill** A pre-Conquest (1066 and all that) body of the church was rebuilt by Wren but the "money ran out before he could repair or rebuild the tower". This was left to his successor, and prodigy, Nicholas Hawksmoor, to complete the task. The church's present Victorian atmosphere was the result of a restoration programme by Scott in the nineteenth century.

G **St Mary Woolnoth** A unique church, being the only one built to the designs of Nicholas Hawksmoor. 'Woolnoth' is likely to be a corruption of 'Wulfnoth', the Saxon founder of the church. After the Great Fire Wren did minor, inadequate repairs, and by the early eighteenth century it was in need of urgent rebuilding. The cost of the rebuilding was met from the funds of the Fifty New Churches Act of 1711.

H **St Clement Eastcheap** Ronnie Ellen in his "A London Steeple chase" wrote, " The church is hard to find partly because it is well hidden,

Bus Route 11: Victoria to Liverpool Street Station   57

partly because it is not in, or even off Eastcheap. When Wren rebuilt it after the fire, it was. But the construction of King William Street in 1829 at the northern end of Eastcheap disappeared. It is now in St Clement's Lane. This is the original church of the nursery rhyme "Oranges and Lemons say the Bells of St Clements". Citrus fruits were unloaded on the riverside wharf within the parish boundary.

I   **The Monument** A constant reminder of the Great Fire of London in 1666. The work of Sir Christopher Wren, it stands 202 feet (66 metres) tall, which is the distance from its base to the point in nearby Pudding Lane where the Fire started in a baker's shop. There are 311 stairs to climb to the balcony. Admission charge payable.

J   **Cannon Street Stations** Designed by John Hawkshaw for the South Eastern Railway Company as their City terminus. During the 1960s most of the site was redeveloped, leaving only the river end untouched.

K   **Tallow Chandlers' Hall** The makers of candles from animal fat rather than the beeswax of the Wax-chandlers. Regulations were made in the Middle Ages forbidding butchers to sell tallow (suet from sheep and cattle) to foreigners, but permitting it to the Company. Today, membership reflects the change of use, with plastics playing an important part.

L   **St Stephen Walbrook** The medieval church was destroyed in the Great Fire and rebuilt by Wren in the 1670s. It is considered to be one of his masterpieces, and the dome a "small sample" for the later one for the cathedral. The church is the founding home of the Samaritans.

M   **Mithraic Temple** One of the greatest archaeological finds in the late 40s and early 50s in the City was the finding of this Temple. It was always assumed that the Cult of Mithras reached London during the Roman occupation. The cult was popular among Roman soldiers after its spread through the Empire from Persia (Iran).

N   **Mansion House** Since the late eighteenth century, the home of the Lord Mayor of London during his term of office. The architect was George Dance, the City Surveyor; it cost over £70,000 and was paid for from the fines of those Aldermen who refused to serve in the Office of Sheriff.

Behind the Bank, in Lothbury, is the parish church of **St Margaret**. First mentioned in the twelfth century, it was rebuilt by Wren after the Great Fire. The interior is full of woodwork, much of it from other, demolished, city churches. The rood screen, one of only two in the City, came from the church of All Hallows the Great in Upper

Thames Street when it was demolished in 1893. Shortly after the Bank, on the corner of Old Broad Street, is the now defunct Stock Exchange Building. Since the "Big Bang" the work previously carried out here has been transferred to the individual offices of the stockbrokers, who now use the latest in Information Technology (IT) in their work.

On the right-hand side of Old Broad Street, over-shadowed by the NatWest tower building, is the City of London Club. Founded in 1832 by bankers, merchants and ship owners, it boasts among its original members the Duke of Wellington, Sir Robert Peel, and Baron Nathan de Rothschild. It is among the most expensive clubs to belong to in London – and one of the most select.

The journey ends at **Liverpool Street (British Rail) Station** that has recently undergone an extensive refurbishment and is well worth a visit. The station stands on the site of the Convent of St Mary of Bethlehem, built originally as the London house for the Bishop of Bethlehem should he ever wish to visit the City. There is no record that he ever did visit! In the early days the sisters ran a hospital, probably for general ailments, but from about 1377 they began to specialise. It became a hospital for mentally "distracted patients" and as such remained under the care of the sisters until the Dissolution of the Monasteries Act of the sixteenth century. At that time the Corporation of London bought the site and continued the work of the sisters. In the following century it moved to larger premises near Moorgate where it remained until the nineteenth century. In 1800 the buildings were declared unsafe, and a fresh plot of land was bought in Lambeth. The new buildings were ready for occupation in 1815, at which time one hundred and twenty-two patients were transferred by Hackney carriages to Lambeth. In the following year, at the Governor's request, a wing was added to cater for the criminally insane. They stayed at Lambeth until 1864 when they were removed to Broadmoor Hospital, near Crowthorne in Berkshire. In 1930 a new hospital was built in Surrey and in 1936, after the demolition of the central block, the building became the home for the Imperial War Museum. Bethlehem, reduced to Bethlem, becomes Bedlam, a title that is generally used either for an asylum or a chaotic state of affairs.

Bus Route 14: Centre Point to Putney Heath

Route   Tottenham Court Road – Charing Cross Road – Cambridge Circus – Shaftesbury Avenue – Piccadilly Circus – Piccadilly – Hyde Park Corner – Knightsbridge – Brompton Road – Onslow Square – Sydney Place – Fulham Road – Fulham Broadway – Fulham Road – Putney Bridge – Approach – Putney Bridge – Putney High Street – Putney Hill – Tibbet's Ride – Putney Heath.

Start   New Oxford Street. Centre Point

Finish   Green Man Public House, Putney Heath

Time   Allow forty-five to fifty minutes for the journey.

Bus No. 14

Return   Either by the No. 14 bus or by taking a No. 93 bus from Wimbledon Park Side (road opposite the Green Man).

Tickets   Travelcard to cover Zones 1 to 3.

The bus stop for our journey, by way of the number 14 bus, is in New Oxford Street, below the giant office block of **Centre Point**. For many years the building remained empty and unsold, having been built as part of a speculative market programme in the 1970s. Its construction made planning history in being among the first to be controlled by the local authority's proviso that it was to be part of a traffic roundabout. The architects were Richard Seifert & Partners whose other buildings dominate the London skyline.

On leaving New Oxford Street, the route passes down Charing Cross Road where Foyle's Bookshop can be seen on the right. This was opened in 1906 by William and Gilbert Foyle who, having failed to secure a post in the Civil Service, advertised their now unwanted textbooks. The response opened out for them an entirely new approach to their futures – the selling of secondhand books. Before his death in 1963, William had built up a stock of books that took miles of shelving to accommodate. "If you cannot find the book you want in Foyle's, then it isn't in London". On the opposite side of the road is **The Phoenix Theatre** which was built in 1930 on the site of the old music-hall The Alcazar. It was designed by Sir Giles Gilbert Scott, the eminent architect, whose other works in London include Waterloo Bridge and the many red telephone boxes.

At the end of the road is Cambridge Circus, a junction of eight roads leading to various parts of the Capital. The circus is dominated by **The Palace Theatre** which opened in 1891 as the Royal English Opera House and was built for Richard D'Oyly Carte. The opening production of an opera, "Ivanhoe" by Sir Arthur Sullivan, was not a success. It lasted only six months, after which the theatre became a music-hall. Since the 1940s the theatre has been the home of many highly successful musicals including "The Song of Norway", "Carissima", and "The King's Rhapsody". Rodgers and Hammerstein's "The Sound of Music" played here from 1961 to 1967 and the current production, "Les Miserables", opened in 1980 and is still going strong.

We leave the Circus by way of Shaftesbury Avenue leading to Piccadilly Circus, although we do not enter it, the bus being diverted down Great Windmill Street to the Haymarket. To the right the streets all lead to **Soho**, a "land of entertainment and food" and well worth a visit! To the left is London's Modern Chinatown that abounds with Chinese food stores and eating places.

Shaftesbury Avenue is part of London's Theatreland with the recently renamed **Gielgud Theatre**, previously the Globe and built in 1906 as the Hicks Theatre, honouring one of England's greatest contemporary actors – Sir John Gielgud. **The Apollo Theatre**, also on the right, was built in 1901 specifically for musical productions. Prior to the First World War, 1914-1918, the theatre was host to The Follies that ran for over five hundred performances. Today the building is used for comedies and straight plays. Finally, next to the Apollo is **The Lyric Theatre**. This was designed by C.J. Phipps in 1888 for the impresario Henry J. Leslie who financed the project from the profit of his highly successful production of the comic opera "Dorothy" at the Prince of Wales Theatre.

At the end of Great Windmill Street, and on the corner of the Haymarket, is Rudy Weller's Horses of Helios – the Sun God complete with cascading water. Look up to the top of the building where there are three divers about to descend into the fountains beneath!

With all the busy traffic in the Haymarket today, it is hard to think that two hundred years ago it was a market where hay was sold. Near to where the bus turns right into Charles II Street, there are two more of London's famous theatres. On the left is the **Theatre Royal, Haymarket**, also known as the Haymarket Theatre, which has an interesting history. It was built originally, on the site next door to the present building, in 1720 by a carpenter called John Porter. Unfortunately, he did not have a licence for professional performances to take place in it. Therefore he could only hire out to amateur actors who did not require a licence to perform their plays. Later the theatre enjoyed royal patronage and was granted a royal licence, hence the Royal in the title. The present building, built alongside the original, was designed by John Nash in the early nineteenth century, after which the first theatre was demolished.

In 1995 Sir John Gielgud unveiled a plaque commemorating Oscar Wilde and his associations with the theatre. This is to be found on the Suffolk (rear) Street wall of the building. On the corner of Charles II Street is **Her Majesty's Theatre**, originally called, in 1704, the Queen's Theatre after Queen Anne. It was designed by Sir John Vanbrugh, the playwright, who was at that time embarking on a new career as an architect. It opened with a production of the Italian opera "The Loves of Ergas" by Thomas Betterton's Company of Players. Vanbrugh's theatre was burnt down in 1789 and was rebuilt by Michael Novosielski exclusively for operatic productions. It was the largest theatre in London and was used by the company from the Drury Lane Theatre while their building was being rebuilt in the late eighteenth century. After a disastrous fire in 1867, the shell was rebuilt in the French Renaissance style by C.J. Phipps in 1869. In 1904 a drama school was started at the theatre which later transferred to Gower Street where it became the Royal Academy of Dramatic Art (RADA).

At the end of Charles II Street the bus turns right into Regent Street. Here, on the right, can be seen the **British Rail Travel Centre**, a useful place to visit for tourist information, books and souvenirs.

At the junction of Regent Street and Piccadilly Circus the bus turns left into **Piccadilly**, traditionally taking its name from Piccadil House, the home of a tailor who designed and made a ruff called a Piccadil. Alternatively, daffodil flowers are also said to have flourished here in earlier times. Today the street is lined with many shops, attracting both the tourist and the Londoner alike. On the left is Simpson (Piccadilly) Ltd, a department store designed by Joseph Emberton. When it was opened in 1936 it was the first welded steel building in London. Its importance as an architectural first has been duly recognised and it is now a listed building, a building of architectural merit.

St James's parish church is Wren's only London church to be built on an entirely new site and was built in 1674. The necessity for having a "new" church here in the seventeenth century came about with the development of the area previously known as St James's Fields which belonged to the estate of St James's Palace. Henry Jermyn, Earl of St Albans, obtained permission to develop the land from a grateful monarch – Charles II. On the right-hand side, at the end of a cul-de-sac, is Albany which was built in the early nineteenth century as a series of chambers for bachelors.

On the corner of Piccadilly and Duke Street St James's is one of London's most famous stores – **Fortnum and Mason Ltd**. William Fortnum came to London in 1704, met Hugh Mason and struck up a friendship with him. After having served in the Household of Queen Anne for a number of years, when he retired he opened a small grocery shop with his friend, Hugh Mason. With Fortnum's knowledge of the royal household and its needs, they soon became established as purveyors of goods, not only to the royals but also to a number of the gentlemen's clubs of St James's. The shop was completely rebuilt between 1923 and 1925. In passing, look for the clock on the Piccadilly side of the building. Placed over the main entrance in 1964, it was designed by Berkeley Sutcliffe and sculptured by P.J. Bentham. The two simulated eighteenth century figures are Mr Fortnum and Mr Mason, on the hour they turn and bow to each other.

Opposite the shop is **Burlington House**, the core of which dates from 1664. Once the home of the Earls of Burlington, it is now the Royal Academy of Arts. Founded in 1768, it is England's oldest society that is solely devoted to the fine arts. George III became its "patron, protector and supporter" and Sir Joshua Reynolds its first President. Other founder members include Benjamin West, the American artist, Thomas Gainsborough and Paul Sandby. Next to Burlington House is the **Burlington Arcade**. The arcade, famous for its shops and tall beadles, was designed by Samuel Ware for Lord Cavendish of Burlington House as a means of preventing "persons unknown" from throwing their rubbish over his garden wall!

Look to the left at the traffic lights. This is St James's Street, leading down to St James's Palace. It is to this royal palace that all foreign ambassadors are accredited on their appointment to serve their country in Great Britain. Although the Queen does not hold court there, they present their Letters of Appointment to her at Buckingham Palace her royal residence. One of London's most famous hotels – The Ritz – is on the left. Built on the site of the former Walsingham House and the Bath Hotel, it is named after the Swiss hotelier who commissioned it. Designed by Mewes and Davis (who also designed the Paris Ritz), the hotel was opened in 1906. It is built of Norwegian granite and Portland stone and was London's first major steel-framed building. Like Simpson's earlier commission along the street, it is a listed building. The word "Ritzy" has now entered the dictionary and has come to mean "high-class, luxurious or ostentatiously smart".

To one side of the hotel is Green Park one of the many green islands in which London abounds. "Green" because there are no formal flower beds in the park, although in recent years daffodils have been 'naturalised'. The main reason for the lack of flowers is that the River Tyburn flowed through the area and created a wet, fen-like landscape in which flowers did not grow. Looking ahead from the bus it is possible to see the dip in the roadway as it enters and leaves the sides of the river. Today the river is beneath the surface, but in early November a river mist still rises out of the line of the river as it passes through the park. At weekends the railings of the park are hung with paintings and other objects of art that are offered for sale.

Piccadilly culminates at Hyde Park Corner. Just before this point, on the right-hand side, is the **Hard Rock Cafe**, a favourite rendezvous for lovers of popular music. **Hyde Park Corner** is one of the busiest road junctions in London and is the meeting place of four major roadways – Park Lane, Piccadilly, Grosvenor Place and Knightsbridge. On the central roundabout are a number of interesting memorials. The tall archway is the Wellington Arch, commemorating the Duke of Wellington, and once stood in front of Buckingham Palace. On the north, right-hand side, is the "David" memorial, the war memorial to members of the Machine Gunner Corps. Nearby is an equestrian statue of the Duke of Wellington with the "Grand Old Duke" sitting on his favourite steed – Copenhagen. Opposite the Arch is the memorial to the gunners of the Royal Artillery.

On the Knightsbridge corner is the Lanesborough Hotel – previously St George's Hospital. The hospital is now housed in a new building in South London. Opposite the hotel is **Hyde Park** which has 138 hectares (340 acres) of open (public) space. Here it is possible to stroll along the paths, enjoy the flower beds in the various seasons of the year, or watch the horse-riders in Rotten Row.

Knightsbridge has shops, apartments, hotels, an embassy or two, as well as the Royal Thames Yacht Club. Nearby is the French Embassy that was built for one of the early financiers of the railways – "Railway Hudson". He made, and lost, a fortune in speculating in railway shares. It was here that Napoleon III held a reception in honour of Queen Victoria when he made an official visit to England. The dominant hotel, on the right, is the Hyde Park Hotel. It was built in the 1880s, by the architects Archer and Green, as an expensive apartment block. Opposite the hotel is Sloane Street with the Knightsbridge Underground Station (Piccadilly Line) on the corner. The roadway now divides. To the right it leads to Kensington Gore, the Royal Albert Hall, Kensington Gardens and Kensington High Street.

Our route is to the left and Brompton Road. Here, on the right, is a narrow short street – Knightsbridge Green. The street is all that is left of the green that occupied the area where the Park Mansions (Scotch Corner) now stand. Here Tattersall's set up their premises in 1864, remaining here until 1939 when they moved to Newmarket. They were among the leading London auctioneers of horses and their premises included two subscription rooms for members of the Jockey Club. It also became a recognised centre for the placing of bets on the turf and a general meeting place for the " racing fraternity". The only reminder of their former presence here is the group of bronze horses on a nearby building.

Harrods' store, Brompton Road

Further down the road on the left is the world-famous **Harrods** Store. The store was founded in 1849 when Henry Charles Harrods, a wholesale tea merchant in the City of London, bought a shop in Knightsbridge. From these small beginnings has grown the vast department store of today. The main part of the present building, designed by Stevens and Munt, was begun in 1901, but not finally completed until 1939 when the Meat Hall was decorated. It has now become one of the largest stores in the world. "There is only one sale and that is Harrods. And it starts on Monday," is an announcement that is made shortly after Christmas every year. On the corners of the building can be seen the "By Appointment" signs of Her Majesty the Queen, H.R.H. Prince Philip, Duke of Edinburgh, Queen Elizabeth the Queen Mother, and H.R.H. Charles, Prince of Wales.

Shortly, on the right, are the **Brompton Oratory**, with the parish church of Holy Trinity, Brompton behind it, and the Victoria & Albert Museum to the side of it. In the sixteenth century St Philip Neri founded the Institute of the Oratory (Oratorians) in Rome. It was a priestly Order which served here from 1847. The Baroque style

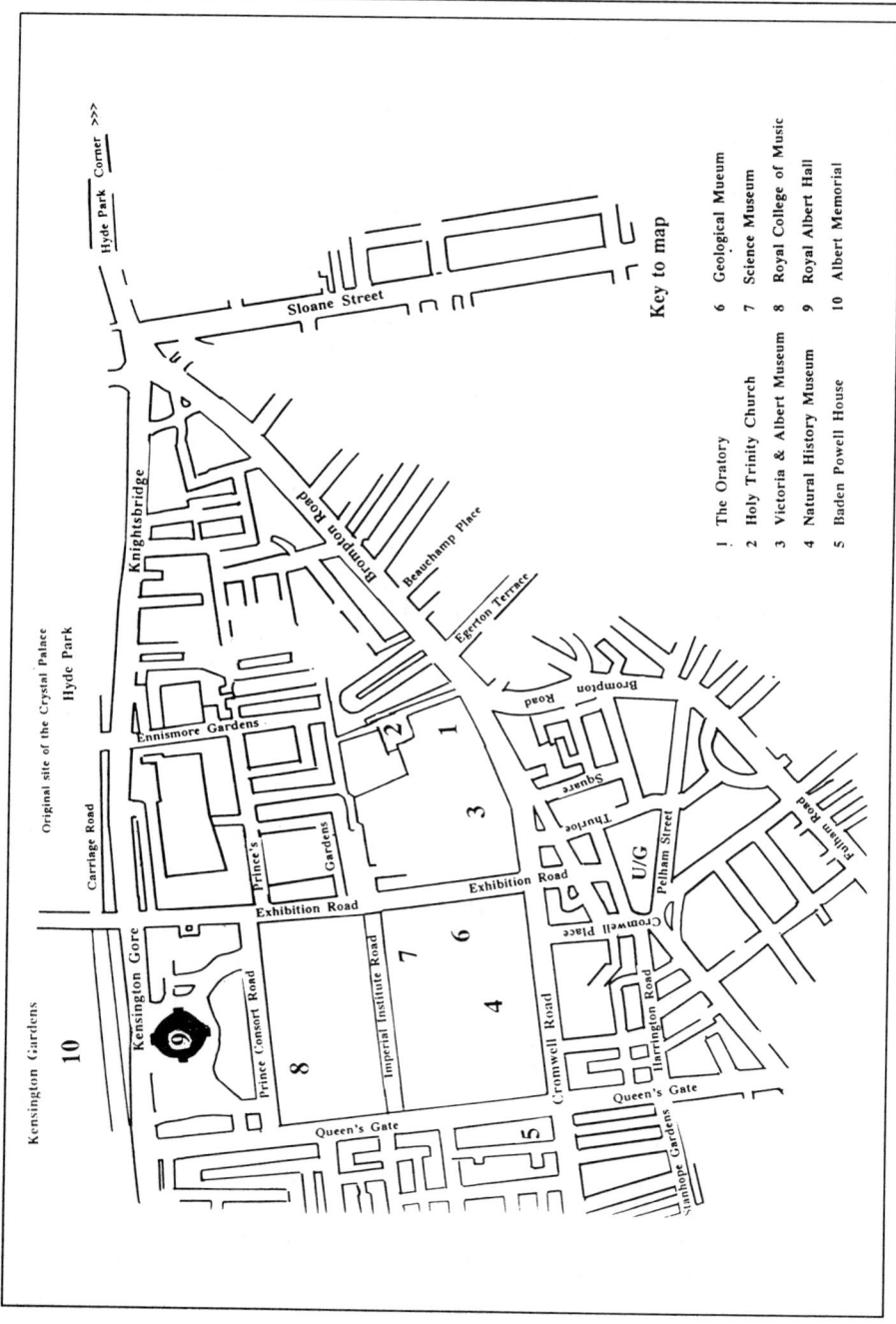

Oratory church was designed by Herbert Gribble and was based on the Mother Church of the Order in Rome. The fittings include the high altar from the church of St Servatius, Maastricht in Belgium and marble statues of the Apostles from Sienna. The road to the side of the Catholic Oratory leads to the Anglican parish church of **Holy Trinity, Brompton**. Work startedon the building in 1826 and the church was consecrated in June 1829. Under the Church Building Act of 1818, a grant of one million pounds was made to the Church (of England) to build extra churches where there was insufficient room in the existing buildings. The Commissioners created by the Act gave a grant of £7,407 towards the total cost of £10,407, the local inhabitants being left to raise the outstanding amount, which they did! The architect was T.L. Donaldson and the builder was Archibald Richie. They produced a plain Gothic-style building of stock (yellow) brick. A strict Evangelical tradition is maintained here with the church packed to capacity for all its services and other activities. It is known far and wide as HTB (Holy Trinity Brompton).

Brompton Oratory's other neighbour is **The Victoria and Albert Museum** which was founded in 1852 as a Museum of Fine and Applied Arts. It settled in South Kensington in 1857 on land that had been bought from the profits of the Great Exhibition of 1851. The exhibition that had been held in Hyde Park had, as its central feature, the Crystal Palace designed by Joseph Paxton. At first the exhibits were housed in wooden sheds, but these were replaced, eventually, by the present building. The foundation stone was laid by Queen Victoria in 1899, who, in her last important public engagement of her reign, and signified that the museum should be called by its present name. However, the building was not completed until 1909 when it was officially opened by Edward VII. A visit to the museum is a must for anyone interested in the Arts.

South Kensington Museums: key to map

1 **The Oratory** Built between 1878 and 1884, it was designed by Herbert Gribble as the result of a competition. It is in the Baroque style of architecture.

2 **Holy Trinity Church** Built in 1829, the church is known as HTB, and is a well-known centre for evangelical teaching. To attend a service arrive early – it always 'plays' to a full house.

3   **Victoria & Albert Museum** Opened in 1852 as the Museum of Manufacturers in Marlborough House along with the School of Design, another forerunner of the Royal College of Art. The building's foundation stone was laid in 1899 by Queen Victoria who named it the Victoria and Albert Museum. The building was opened by her son, Edward VII on 26th June 1909.

4   **Natural History Museum** At a special general meeting of the Trustees of the British Museum in January 1860 it was proposed, and passed, that the Natural History Collection should be removed to separate premises in South Kensington. The building, by Alfred Waterhouse, was opened in 1881.

5   **Baden Powell House Museum** The museum, in the Scout International hostel, illustrates the life of Lord Baden Powell, the founder of the Boy Scouts. Items include the manuscript of "Scouting for Boys", and a loaf of bread baked during the siege of Mafeking in 1899.

6   **Geological Museum** Originally the Museum of Economic Geology housed in Craig's Court off Whitehall. It moved to South Kensington in 1935.

7   **Science Museum** In 1852 it was opened in Marlborough House as the Museum of Ornamental and was the museum of the Central School of Practical Art. The school is now the Royal College of Art.

8   **Royal College of Music** Founded in 1882 at a meeting called by the Prince of Wales (later Edward VII), with George Grove, compiler of the "Dictionary of Music", its first Director. The building was designed by Sir Arthur Blomfield in 1894.

9   **Royal Albert Hall** After a number of false starts, the Hall was designed by Captain Fowke in 1865 as a memorial to Prince Albert, Prince Consort to H.M. Queen Victoria, on a site owned by the Great Exhibition Commissioners. A peppercorn rent of one shilling (5p) a year was to be paid annually on the 25th March – and it still is!

10 **Albert Memorial** In 1862 a meeting was convened by the Lord Mayor of London, William Cubitt, to discuss proposals to erect a memorial to the late Prince Consort. After a limited competition George Gilbert Scott's designs were accepted and used. Today, the construction is "under wraps" with a massive restoration programme in progress. If all goes well it will be un-wrapped in the Millennium.

From Brompton Road the route passes South Kensington Underground Station, a useful station to use when visiting the museums in the area. Then, by way of Onslow Square and Sydney Place, it enters Fulham Road. It was at 36 Onslow Square that the writer William Makepeace Thackeray lived at the time he founded the "Cornhill Magazine". His last two novels were published in monthly instalments in the magazine.

Fulham Road was once a coaching road that led to Portsmouth and was noted for the numerous footpads that frequented it. Early maps show it marked as being either the King's Highway or the London Road. On the corner of Old Church Street stands a public house called The Queen's Elm. This is the successor of The Queen's Tree tavern that is said to commemorate an elm tree under which Elizabeth I sheltered in a rain storm. Further along the road, on the right-hand side, is an entrance to the **Brompton Cemetery**. Founded in 1840, it covers some 16 hectares (39 acres), is owned by the Department of the Environment, and is rated among the finest of London's cemeteries. Among the famous persons buried here are Francis Fowke, architect of the Royal Albert Hall, and George Borrow, author, whose writings include "The Romany Rye" and the "Bible in Spain". The latter is a reminder that he was for many years an agent for the British and Foreign Bible Society. The first Director of the Victoria and Albert Museum, Sir Henry Cole, and William Bunting, the royal undertaker of the nineteenth century are also buried here.

Shortly after passing over the Stamford Brook on the right-hand side are the stadium and grounds of the **Chelsea Football Club** – "The Blues". Founded in 1905, they have won a number of championships since that time. The site of the club's grounds was once a market garden, and the nearby railway lines follow the line of the former Stamford Brook. According to tradition the club's conception was over a pint (or two!) of beer in a Fulham Public House. The selection of a name for the club caused problems as there was already a Fulham Football Club. To call it the London Football Club was slightly pretentious, so after much discussion Chelsea was chosen. That particular borough did not boast a club of its own.

Just past the football ground, on the right, is the Sir Oswald Stoll Foundation for Disabled Servicemen which was founded after the

First World War to cater for those men who suffered injury during that conflict. The parish church of St John, Walham Green, stands on an island where the village green used to be. The only green now is the churchyard around the church. Built in 1828 to the designs of J.H. Taylor, the building was erected on the site of the former village pond. Fulham Road continues past the church to a Catholic Convent and School on the corner of Kelvedon Road. The school was founded in 1895 and is run by the Sisters of the Holy Name of Mary. The Catholic Order was founded by Pere Colin, who also founded the Society of Mary in Lyons in 1816, to teach girls and to work with the Fathers on the missions.

At the end of the road is Fulham High Street with The King's Head public house. Behind this is The Warren, part of the grounds of Fulham Palace.

To the right, as the bus approaches Putney Bridge by way of Putney Bridge Approach, can be seen the parish church of All Saints, Putney which was rebuilt in the nineteenth century in the style of the Middle Ages. Beyond the church is the former palace of the Bishops of London. It now houses a museum and may also be hired for conferences and other functions. Conducted tours are arranged from time to time. The grounds are generally open as a public park and are well worth a visit.

The first **Putney Bridge** was built of timber in 1727 by Thomas Phillips, and for fifty years it was the only bridge across the River Thames west of London Bridge in the City of London. The present bridge by Sir Joseph Bazalgette, the engineer responsible for the embankments of the City of London and Westminster, was opened in 1886. Since 1845 the annual Oxford and Cambridge boat race has started from the upstream (left-hand side) of the bridge. At the end of the bridge is the parish church of St Mary, Putney. The earliest mention of the church is in 1291. The tower, which was restored in 1836 when the rest of the church was rebuilt, is fourteenth century.

Putney High Street, a busy shopping centre, leads to Putney Hill and our destination – Putney Heath. At 11 Putney Hill, Algernon Swinburne, essayist and critic, lived with his friend, Theodore Watts-Dunton. The heath comprises some 160 hectares (400 acres) and it is difficult to define where the heath ends and Wimbledon Common begins. They merge into one another somewhere beyond the King's Mere (pond). Perhaps before strolling over the Heath there might be time to visit The Green Man public house, just opposite to where the bus stops.

An alternative return journey would be to board a number 93 bus to Wimbledon Station where the District Line of the underground railway or British Rail trains take their passengers back to central London.

Bus Route 15: Paddington to the Tower of London (Aldgate)

Route Praed Street – Edgware road – Marble Arch – Oxford Street – Oxford Circus – Regent Street – Piccadilly Circus – Haymarket – Pall Mall East – Trafalgar Square – Duncannon Street - Strand – Aldwych – Strand – Temple Bar – Fleet Street – Ludgate Hill – St Paul's Churchyard South – Cannon Street – Eastcheap – Great Tower Street – Trinity Square – Tower of London – Aldgate – "Petticoat Lane" (Middlesex Street).

Start Praed Street, outside the Post Office building.

Finish Tower of London **or** Aldgate

Time Allow forty-five minutes for the journey.

Bus No. 15

Return Either by bus 15 or from Tower Hill underground station. If visiting Petticoat Lane Market, then bus 15 and Aldgate underground station.

Tickets Travelcard covering Zones 1 & 2.

Paddington, one of the "lost villages" of London, still retains its eighteenth century church – on Paddington Green. It is a short walk from the bus stop in Praed Street where we begin our journey to the Tower of London.

As soon as the bus moves away from the stop, on the left is St Mary's Hospital. Opened in 1851, its buildings were progressively built during the latter part of the nineteenth century. In 1928 Alexander Fleming, working in a laboratory here, discovered the significance of penicillin. A "purple plaque" can be seen on the wall at the end of the building commemorating Fleming's work. The laboratory is now a small museum dedicated to Alexander Fleming, and is open to the general public. Praed Street is named after William Praed, a banker and Chairman of the Grand Junction Canal Company. The Paddington Basin of the canal is situated behind the buildings on the left-hand side of the roadway. Opened in 1820, the basin links the Regent Canal with the Grand Junction and finally becomes part of the Grand Union Canal. It is possible to travel by water from Paddington to the heart of Birmingham some hundred miles away.

From Praed Street, the bus turns right into the Edgware Road. Built on the line of the former Roman Watling Street, today's roadway is a busy shopping thoroughfare. Sussex Gardens, on the right at the cross-roads, was built in the eighteenth century, privately, as London's first by-pass and called "The New Road". It was built as a means of getting the cattle to the abattoirs of Smithfield Market after numerous complaints from the ladies and gentlemen whose journeys to the City were seriously impeded by the cattle. A toll was imposed on those using the roadway. This did not deter the ladies and gentlemen from using it once they too found it quicker to travel to the City by way of the road. So the original purpose for building the road was soon defeated. Humans and animals enjoyed each other's company once again!

At the end of Edgware Road can be seen Hyde Park, and on the road island, on the right, a round stone plaque marking the site of the notorious Tyburn Tree. It stood 3 metres (11ft) high, had three sides, each 2.5 metres (8ft) in length, and was used to "hang, draw and quarter" countless criminals, traitors and Christian martyrs from the fourteenth to the eighteenth centuries. A short walk along Bayswater Road is the Roman Catholic Benedictine Convent where the enclosed community of nuns constantly prays for the repose of the souls of the Catholic Martyrs of the sixteenth and seventeenth centuries. The bus now passes **Marble Arch** on the right. Built originally to the designs of John Nash as an entrance gateway to Buckingham Palace, it was moved here in 1851. Rumour has it that the state coaches could not pass safely through the central archway! Eighteenth century maps mark the site as a milestone for distances to and from the City.

Oxford Street lies ahead. Maps over the years have labelled the street by various titles. In the early seventeenth century it was shown as "The Waye from Uxbridge", in 1678 as "The King's Highway", "The Oxford Road" in 1682 and "The Acton Road" in 1691. At various other times it was simply known as "The Tyburn Way" being a route along which those condemned to death in Newgate Prison journeyed to meet their end on "The Tree". Many people who come to London will want to go shopping in Oxford Street. Here can be seen, and visited (!), many world famous shops including: Marks and Spencer's, Lilley & Skinner and Peter Robinson. The first started as a "penny market" in Leeds market place in 1884. A sign over the stall read "Marks's Penny Market – Don't Ask the Price – It's a Penny". The Marble Arch branch, lovingly known as "No.1 Marks and Sparks", was opened in 1930. Lilley and Skinner, on the corner of Stafford Place, is one of the largest specialist shoe shops in the world, while Peter Robinson, at Oxford Circus, concentrates on women's fashion accessories. Founded in 1833, the store was completely rebuilt in 1967 on two floors. D.H. Evans was founded by a Welshman from Llanelly in 1879. The present building was erected between 1936 and 1937. It sells men's wear. John Lewis was a Somerset man, born in Shepton Mallett, and was a draper's apprentice in Wells before coming to London and starting his own business in Holles Street. His son, John Spedan Lewis, created the immense business empire of today. The store's boast is "never knowingly undersold". C & A has been owned by a Dutch family, the Brenninkmeyers, since 1841. They specialise in selling up-to-the-minute fashions to the mass market.

Today's street offers the visitor and the Londoner alike the chance to visit some, or all, of the many shops that line the roadway. In March 1909 Selfridge's Limited was opened. It was the brainchild of Harry Gordon Selfridge who was born in Ripon, Wisconsin, U.S.A. in 1857. After setting up and running a highly successful store in Chicago for a number of years, he sold out and moved to England. When Gordon Selfridge was building his store he had the idea of connecting it with Bond Street underground (subway) station. He even suggested that the station be renamed "Selfridges" – it wasn't! When he first mooted the idea he met with opposition from the authorities, and a natural obstacle in the form of an underground river. The builders of the station also met the river, the Tyburn, that still flows from Hampstead in North London down to the River Thames at Westminster. Part of the tunnel is still in use in the basement floor of the shop. When his own tunnel foundered, Selfridge became an ardent supporter of the proposal of building a tunnel under the English Channel! An artesian well under the building was linked to a fountain in the centre of the store. It was rumoured that the water had medicinal powers. This led to shoppers bringing bottles with them when they shopped to collect the waters. However, when the Metropolitan Water Board heard of this activity they threatened to put a meter on it and charge. This, too, was stopped. So began one of London's most famous stores – Selfridge's. When he died in 1947 at the age of ninety the store became his memorial. The building was designed by a young Paris-trained American architect, Daniel Burnham, and was erected under the supervision of R.F. Atkinson, an English architect.

The side roads of Oxford Street are many and devious, leading to corners of London that lend themselves to being explored, on foot, at a later date. Duke Street, on the left, leads to Manchester Square where can be seen the Wallace Collection of European and English paintings and a fine collection of Oriental and European Armour. They are housed in the former Hertford House, built in the eighteenth century and opened as a national museum by the Prince of Wales, later Edward VII, in 1900. Stratford Place leads to the former Stratford House, built in the 1770s by Richard Edwin, the architect, and now the Oriental Club. The Club was founded in 1824 by officers who had served on the staff of the East India Company, but were not eligible for membership of one of the popular military clubs of London. The present day members do not necessarily have any direct connection with the Orient. At number 7, Martin Van Buren, the eighth President of the United States of America, lived when he was that country's Ambassador to the Royal Court of St James. The brick building on the corner is a former Watch House that was used by the parish watchmen during their spell of duty in patrolling the streets.

Oxford Circus marks the meeting point of four roadways. Here the bus turns right down Regent Street and soon passes Hamley's, the "largest toy shop in the world". Founded by William Hamley as "Noah's Ark" in Holborn, it moved here in 1906. From early days the store was a ready haven for inventors of board games and similar goods, who inevitably offered them to Mr Hamley for approval. Parallel to Regent Street, behind the buildings on the left-hand side, is **Carnaby Street**. The street rose to fame in 1957 when the Capital's first boutique for men was opened here. The Oxford English Dictionary acknowledges Carnaby Street as a mecca for fashionable clothing for young people. Regent Street was laid out by John Nash in 1823 as part of the proposed processional route from Carlton House (now Carlton Terrace) to Regent's Park. However, on the death of the Prince of Wales's father, George III, in 1820, the plans for a new palace in the Park were dropped. Towards the Piccadilly end of the street, on the left, is Aquascutum's shop. They were exhibitors at the Great Exhibition of 1851 in Hyde Park where they proudly displayed their recently patented showerproof material.

In **Piccadilly Circus** there are several points of interest for the tourist to see, perhaps the best known being the memorial water fountain that stands on the pavement in front of the Criterion Theatre. Popularly called **Eros**, it is more correctly the Shaftesbury Memorial Fountain. Designed by Alfred Gilbert, it was erected by public subscription and commemorates the philanthropic 7th Earl of Shaftesbury. It's the Angel of Christian Charity and not Eros the Greek God of Love, whose arrow (shaft) has left his bow and buried itself in the ground. That is – Shaftes plus bury, a rebus or play on the good earl's name. It was unveiled in 1894 and was the first aluminium statue in London, and originally had drinking cups for the use of thirsty passers-by. They were stolen and not replaced!

Number One, Piccadilly Circus is the former theatre, music hall and cinema – the London Pavilion. It now houses the **Madame Tussaud's Rock Circus** and **Rock Island Diner**, as well as shops and services to meet the needs of tourists and visitors to London. Londoners themselves are also attracted to the building and enjoy all that it provides. A niche on the corner of Haymarket and Piccadilly houses Rudy Weller's "House of Helios", the Sun God, complete with cascading water. It has been estimated that some fifty to sixty million people pass by them every year – on buses and on foot.

In the Haymarket there are two of London's famous theatres. On the left, **"The Theatre Royal"** and **"Her Majesty's Theatre"** on the right. The former was rebuilt by John Nash in 1820-1821 on the site of the eighteenth century building that had become derelict. "Her Majesty's", the home of many musical productions, was designed by C.J. Phipps and opened in 1897. At the side of the theatre, the Carlton Hotel was built at the same time. This was demolished in 1957 to make room for New Zealand House. This eighteen storey office block was designed by Robert Matthew for the New Zealand High Commission and opened by Elizabeth II in 1963.

Nelson's Column

Pall Mall East, at the end of the Haymarket, leads into **Trafalgar Square**, with **The National Gallery** on the left. Designed by William Wilkins, the gallery took six years to complete between 1832 and 1838. It was built to house the paintings of John Julius Angerstein, a Russian merchant and philanthropist. It is known familiarly to many Londoners as the "national cruet set" after the three domes that adorn the roof of the gallery. The gallery houses many paintings from various schools, including English, Spanish, Flemish and Dutch. However, the prime home for British art is the Tate Gallery on Millbank. The site of the National Gallery is where once the Kings kept their hunting birds. The noise from these birds, particularly in the mating season, gave rise to the stables here being called "Mews" from their mewing.

Standing on the top of his 43 metres (140ft) column, on the south side of the square, is Horatio, Lord Nelson. The square commemorates his finest, and last, great sea-battle, on the 21st October 1805, off the coast of Spain near Cape Trafalgar. Originally it was suggested that his ship *HMS Victory* should be floated up the River Thames and put into a dry dock here. The committee changed its mind and settled for a square, fountains and the column.

The bus stops in Duncannon Street at the side of the parish church of **St Martin-in-the Fields**. The church was rebuilt in 1726 to the designs of James Gibbs and is the third building on this site. Originally there had been a small chapel for the use of the monks of Westminster Abbey when they were tending their vegetable garden here – Co(n)vent Garden. The first parish church was commissioned by Henry VIII who, it is said, disliked seeing countless funeral processions passing his palace at Westminster on their way to the church by the Abbey. It is the parish church for Buckingham Palace and any baptism, marriage or funeral services held there are recorded in this church's registers. George I showed great interest in the present building and contributed heavily towards the cost. The interior has one of the finest plaster work ceilings in London and was the work of Artari and Bagutti, the Italian plasterers.

From the church stop the Strand is soon reached, with **Charing Cross** (British Rail and London Underground) Stations ahead. The station was opened in 1864 and was designed by the engineer John Hawkshaw. During the late 1980s new modernistic offices designed by the Terry Quinlan Partnership were built above the platforms. In the forecourt of the station is a replica of the Charing Cross that used to be at the head of Whitehall, where the statue of Charles I now stands. The Cross was the last of a series of crosses erected to commemorate where the body of Eleanor, Edward I's first wife, rested on its way to burial in Westminster Abbey.

In the Strand are two more of London's theatres. The first is **"The Adelphi"** that dates from its last rebuilding in 1930 by Ernest Schaufelberg. It was the setting for the much-loved C.B. Cochrane's Revues in the 1930s and 1940s. A short distance away is **"The Vaudeville Theatre"**, which will be forever linked with the name of Henry Irving, the nineteenth century actor. He performed here in James Albery's "Two Roses" at the opening in 1870. Earlier in this century, Seymour Hicks and his wife, Ellen Terry, acted in a series of plays which ran for a long time. Here "Salad Days" was first performed to packed audiences. At the end of this stretch of the Strand lies the Aldwych, a half circle created by the end of Kingsway being divided around the offices. It was once one of London's worse slum areas that was redesigned at the turn of the century to create new roads to help the flow of traffic in the area.

On the corner of Catherine Street stands **"The Strand Theatre"**, built in 1905 by W.G.R. Sprague, it opened with a series of Italian operas. In the height of the London Blitz of the Second World War, 1940-1941, the late Sir Donald Wolfit, whose Shylock in Shakespeare's "Merchant of Venice" is still remembered affectionately, performed Shakespeare's plays for lunch-time audiences. In the flat above the theatre lived Ivor Novello, the composer and actor who died in 1951. A Greater London Council plaque records his residence here. A matching theatre, **"The Aldwych"**, is on the next corner, just beyond the Waldorf Hotel. This is also the work of W.G.R. Sprague. It was built between 1903 and 1908, when it opened with "Blue Belle in Fairyland" with Seymour Hicks and his wife playing the leading roles. It was also the home, between 1925 and 1933, for the Ben Travers farces. For a time in the 1960s the Royal Shakespeare Company used this theatre as their London base. They are now based in the Barbican Theatre.

Where the Aldwych rejoins the Strand stands the church of **St Clement Danes**, now the Central Church of the Royal Air Force, and said by many to be the original church of the nursery rhyme "Oranges and Lemons". Others dispute the story. St Clement is the patron saint of sailors and it seems appropriate that the sea-faring race of Danes should adopt him when they settled here in the ninth century.

After the Great Fire of London in 1666, the church was rebuilt by Sir Christopher Wren, but the steeple was added later by James Gibbs. During the Second World War the church was gutted, and its bells came tumbling down. All was desolate until 1958 when it was rededicated in the presence of members of the royal family as the church of the RAF. Towards the end of March each year children from the parish school attend a service here at the end of which they are all given an orange and a lemon. Some traditions linger on.

Until the thirteenth century the Royal Law Courts moved around the country with the King. When Edward I came to the throne in 1272 he decided that this was not a good practice. He leased to the "men of Law and their Students" the Great Hall of his Royal Palace at Westminster. Then, in the late nineteenth century, it was decided that the "men of Law" should have their own buildings. A competition for their design was held and won by George Edmund Street. His buildings stand on the left-hand side of the roadway, opposite the east end of the church. Look for the three statues at the end of the Great Hall. In the centre stands Christ with his hand raised in blessing, with Solomon on his right and Alfred the Great on his left. Christ represents the Law of the New Covenant, Solomon the Old Covenant and it is King Alfred from whom the basis of our English Law is said to come.

Standing in the centre of the roadway is a monument surmounted by a dragon – this is the boundary mark of the City of London. In former times Temple Bar stood here and marked the extreme boundary of the jurisdiction of the Lord Mayors of London. Here kings and queens are always met by the Lord Mayor who presents them with the Sword of State of the City. After touching the hilt, the sword is retrieved by the Lord Mayor. The City Marshall then escorts the monarch into the City. The last structure on this site was taken down in 1878 because it got in the way of the traffic! It was rebuilt as the gateway into the grounds of the mansion of the Meux Family at Cheshunt in Hertfordshire, where it remains to this day, although there have been several plans to return it to the City.

Passing the bar allows one to enter into Fleet Street, once the home of all the national newspapers, all of whom have moved away from "The Street". Opposite Chancery Lane, on the left, is Prince Henry's Room. It was built in the early seventeenth century as a meeting place for the Council of the Principality of Wales. Today the first floor room houses a collection of Samuel Pepys, the diarist, memorabilia belonging to the Samuel Pepys Club of London. Note, in passing, the fleur-de-lys and the motto "Ich Dien" – "I serve" – carved in wood on the front of the building. The room is open to the public Mondays to Fridays from 11am to 2pm. Admission is free.

St Dunstan-in-the-West parish church on the left dates from 1831 when the architect, John Shaw, replaced the previous building that had to be demolished to widen Fleet Street. In addition to Anglican worship, some seven orthodox churches regularly use the church for their own services. There is also a shrine to the Polish (Catholic) Church here. The church is the centre for the Church of England's Council on Foreign Affairs. Its seventeenth century clock on the outside of the church has two ancient warriors whose clubs strike out the hours. In the eighteenth century, William Cowper wrote of the warriors:

Bus Route 15: Paddington to the Tower of London (Aldgate)

> "When Labour and when Dullness, club in hand,
> Like the two figures of St Dunstan's stand,
> Beating alternatively in measured time
> The clockwork tinntinnabulum rhyme
> Exact and regular the sound will be,
> But such mere quarter chimes are not for me"

After passing the end of Fetter Lane, on the left, the roadway shows a distinct slope downhill, and at the same time the magnificent cathedral of St Paul's comes into full view. Just before reaching the end of the street, on the right, a glimpse of the parish church of **St Bride's** can be seen. Dedicated to the sixth century Irish Saint Bridget, the medieval church was destroyed in the Great Fire of 1666 and rebuilt to the designs of Sir Christopher Wren. It was bombed during the last war and has since been superbly restored. During the restoration the nave was excavated and many items of interest to historians and archaeologists were brought to light. Many of these are now in the museum in the crypt of the church.

The route has now reached Ludgate Circus where, on the left-hand corner, there is a memorial to Edgar Wallace, author and playwright, who, as a young man, sold newspapers here.

Ahead lies Ludgate Hill and the City Proper – that is the City of London contained within the city walls (alas long since pulled down). Half way up the hill is the parish church of **St Martin-within-Ludgate**, rebuilt by Wren in the latter half of the seventeenth century after the Fire. Traditionally the church is said to have been founded by Cadwalla in the seventh century. As the Chronicler Robert of Gloucester writes:

> "A church of Sent Martyn liuyng he let rere,
> In which yat men should goddys seruyse do,
> And sing for his soul and all Christen also."

At the top of the hill stands the Cathedral Church of **St Paul** in the City of London in all its glory. The present church is the fourth on the site, the first being a converted pagan temple dedicated to the goddess of the Hunt – Diana. This is certainly Christopher Wren's masterpiece, but from the bus we catch only a glimpse. It is worth breaking the journey here to spend some time inside. (There is an admission charge in operation). Opposite the cathedral, on the south (right) side, is the **City of London Information Centre**. Here is a storehouse of information regarding the city. A new choir school at the west end of the cathedral was built between 1962 and 1967 by Leo de Syllas of the Architects Co-Partnership. It replaces the nineteenth century school buildings in Carter Lane. The tower of the building was part of the church of St Augustine, Watling Street that was not rebuilt after the Second World War.

Shortly after the cathedral, the street becomes Cannon Street and is a reminder that the candle makers of medieval London manufactured their wares here. The name is a corruption of Candlewick Street. They were driven out by the City authorities after complaints were lodged against them for making an unacceptable smell with their boiling wax.

At the street's junction with Queen Victoria Street the route lies ahead with the continuation of Cannon Street. On the right Cannon Street Railway and underground stations can be seen. Opposite, in the wall of the North China Bank, behind a wrought iron grille, is London Stone. This is one of London's strangest landmarks and is passed by thousands of people every day who have no idea of its origins. It is a large mass of stone that was probably part of a milliarium (milestone) used to measure distances to and from Roman London (Londinium). A mile equals one thousand paces of a Roman soldier, hence a milestone is a marker for each and every thousand paces. Shakespeare refers to the stone in "Henry VI, Part One" when the rebel leader (Jack Cade) strikes the stone and declares, "Mortimer is now Lord of the City". Other authorities refer to the Stone as being part of a Druid temple said to have been erected at the junction of Cornhill and Leadenhall Street – but that is a different story! Whatever its origins, the stone is an ancient part of the City of London's long and interesting history. A series of roadways merge at the end of Cannon Street, but the bus route lies straight ahead to Eastcheap.

On the left can be seen the Guild Church of St Margaret Pattens, rebuilt by Sir Christopher Wren after the Great Fire. The suffix is said to have been taken from the pattin makers who worked in the area in former times. "Pattins" were raised metal platforms that were tied underneath the sole of the shoe. This enabled the wearer to walk over the rubbish that littered the streets of the City in earlier times. After the church comes Great Tower Street, and finally Byward Street and the parish church of **All-Hallows-by-the-Tower**. There has been a church on this site since the ninth century and evidence of this was found when restoration work was being carried out. A Saxon archway was found in the base of the tower, near to the entrance to the baptistery, but the site is older than the church of the Saxons. Underneath there were the remains of a Roman villa. In the crypt (underground chamber) there is a portion of the mosaic floor of the villa. Conducted visits to the crypt, accompanied by a member of the staff, are often arranged. The church is also the Mother Church of the Toc H Movement started by the late Reverend "Tubby" Clayton during the First World War, 1914-1918, in a chapel at Poperinghe, near Ypres, Belgium. At the close of the war, a fellowship between Christians of all denominations had grown to such strength that the Movement continued – and it still does today.

Across the roadway from the church stands The Tower of London. More correctly Her Majesty's Royal Palace and Armouries of the Tower of London, it dates from the time of William the Conqueror. The king ordered that a tower – the White Tower – should be built on the edge of the city to protect it from possible attack. It is interesting to note that the Tower has never fallen to a foreign power. The Crown Jewels of England are now housed in specially converted rooms of the former Waterloo Barracks. Some two to three hundred people live within the walls of the precincts of the Tower. Among the residents are the Yeoman Warders, all of whom are retired long-serving members of the Armed Forces. The Warders regularly conduct parties of interested visitors around parts of the Tower. For the macabre visitor, there is the site of the execution block and a display of implements of torture. A walk along the upper walkway from the Wakefield Tower to the Brick Tower gives an interesting view of the precincts. The Tower is not to be taken hurriedly, but casually in order to savour some of its atmosphere.

A short journey on from the Tower, a visit to the world famous **Petticoat Lane Market** is well worthwhile on a Sunday morning. Situated close to Aldgate underground station, it takes its name from the market in earlier times that specialised in the sale of ladies' petticoats. Today almost everything is sold here, not only on Sundays, but during the week as well. It is most interesting on Sundays, but if you arrive after lunchtime you will be disappointed, unless you wish to witness the efficiency of the local authority's ability to clear up the debris of the market and to leave it clean and tidy for Monday!

Bus Route 16: Victoria to Kilburn

Route Victoria Station Bus Station – Victoria Street – Grosvenor Gardens – Hyde Park Corner – Park Lane – Marble Arch – Edgware Road – Maida Vale – Kilburn High Road – Kilburn High Road (BR) Station.

Start Victoria Bus Station in British Rail station forecourt.

Finish Kilburn High Road.

Time Allow fifteen minutes for the journey.

Bus No. 16

Return By No. 16 bus to return to Victoria Station, or buses 16, 16a, and 98 to return to Marble Arch and Oxford Street.

Tickets Travelcard Zones 1 & 2.

The bus station is in front of the railway terminus at Victoria and is divided by boarding platforms for the various buses that use the terminus. No. 16 departs from the platform by the side of the small information office from where useful maps may be obtained.

On leaving the station, the bus enters Victoria Street, on the way passing **Little Ben,** a 10 metre (30ft) version of St Stephen's Clock Tower of the Houses of Parliament. The inscriptions on the side of the clock tower read:

"Little Ben"
First erected in 1892. Taken down 1964.
Restored and re-erected on the 15th December 1981
By the Westminster City Council
With the help of ELF Aquitaine UK
Offered as a gesture of Franco-British Friendship.
Little Ben's apology for Summer Time
My hands you may retard or may advance
My heart beats true for England as for France
JWR
Restored and rebuilt
1981
by
John Smith & Sons
Midland Clock Works Ltd.,
Derby

Opposite the clock tower is **"The Victoria Palace"** theatre. The present building was opened in November 1911 as a music-hall. The site was previously occupied by Moy's Music Hall, and later by the Royal Standard Music Hall, Pimlico. It was for a number of years one of the most popular music-halls in London. Today, it still enjoys much of that former popularity with musicals still being produced here. It was here in 1937 that the ever-popular "Me and My Girl" was first produced. Another popular show, staged here during the Second World War, was "Meet Me Victoria". Doubtless many people did and enjoyed a few hours respite from the horrors of war.

On the left, in Grosvenor Gardens, can be seen the equestrian statue of Marshal Foch. It is a copy of one that stands in Cassel where the Marshal had his Flanders headquarters during the First World War, 1914-1918. A fellow officer once spoke of his "luminosity which quite spiritualises a face that otherwise would be almost brutal, with its great moustache and protruding jaw". As the Commander-in-Chief of the Allied forces he received the German surrender. In the second half of the gardens, at number 26, are the offices of the London Tourist Board and Convention Bureau whose Tourist Information Centre alongside Victoria Station is a mine of information on both London and tourism in general. Unlike the first portion of the gardens that are open to the public to enjoy, these gardens are private. They have in recent years been attractively planted with flowers that are left undisturbed. However, the site has a more macabre story from the past. It was here that highwaymen and other felons were executed and later buried. This did not please the King who ordered the practice to cease! On the diagonally opposite corner is an entrance to the grounds of Buckingham Palace. On the corner, to the left of the traffic lights, stands the memorial to the men of the King's Royal Rifles Corps who lost their lives in the two World Wars.

On the right is the wall of the gardens of **Buckingham Palace**, the London home of Her Majesty the Queen. It is the second largest private garden in Europe, second only to the Pope's garden in the Vatican City. During the summer months a series of garden parties are held here. The area behind the buildings to the left is Belgravia, the home of a number of embassies and some of London's best-kept houses. To walk in there is to step back into the world of the nineteenth century – but, alas, invaded by the motor car!

Ahead lies **Hyde Park Corner**, the busiest road junction in London and one that is surrounded by buildings, statues and monuments of national and international interest. On the left is the Lanesborough Hotel at the end of Knightsbridge. The original building was the home of James Lane, 2nd Viscount Lanesborough, and it was built in 1719. It was bought by a group of dissenting physicians and surgeons of the Westminster Infirmary in 1733. The infirmary was the first London hospital to be supported by voluntary contributions and was opened in 1720. A group of the Governors of the Infirmary considered their original building in Petty France inadequate for their growing needs. Their decision to rent Lanesborough House was partly based on their need for more room, but also because they considered the country air at Knightsbridge:

" in the general opinion of the physicians would be more effectual than physick in the cure of distempers, especially such as mainly affect the poor, who live in close and confined places within these great cities."

On the road island to the right stands The Royal Artillery memorial, with its field gun pointing skywards and at such an angle that should it be capable of firing a shell, it would land in the heart of the Battle of the Somme where thousands of gunners died in the trenches of the First World War. The equestrian statue of the Duke of Wellington stands looking towards Apsley House. Designed by J.E. Boehm, it shows the Duke sitting on his favourite horse, Copenhagen. At the four corners of the plinth stand soldiers representing regiments with which the Iron Duke was associated. The north side shows the 1st Guards and the 42nd Royal Highlanders, and the south the 23rd Royal Welsh Fusiliers and the 6th Inniskilling Dragoons.

A bronze figure of David by Francis Derwent Wood commemorates the "glorious heroes of the Machine Gun Corps who fell in the Great War, 1914-1919". The Biblical text reads: *"Saul that slain his thousands, but David tens of thousands."* On the far side from the hotel is the Wellington Arch designed by Decimus Burton and erected in 1828 as a memorial to the Iron Duke. The statue of Wellington that was placed on the top was later removed to Aldershot. At the present time a bronze group, The Quadriga, by Adrian Jones, a former officer in the 3rd Hussars, stands proudly in its place.

Decimus Burton was also responsible for the stone screen at the side of Apsley House. It was built as a triumphal entrance into Hyde

Park. Apsley House, on the left, houses the Wellington Museum. Known as "No. 1 London", from the time when it was the first house on the western approaches to London, it was built between 1771 and 1778 by Robert Adam for Baron Apsley, later 2nd Earl Bathurst, and bought by Lord Wellesley, Wellington's elder brother. In 1817 the Duke paid his brother £42,000 for the house and commissioned Benjamin Dean Wyatt to add a large dining room to the building. It was in this room that the famous Waterloo Dinners were held.

At the end of the house, the bus turns left into Park Lane. This runs alongside Hyde Park, passing, en route, on the left, gates dedicated to Queen Elizabeth the Queen Mother "after the great show of public affection generated on the occasion of Her Majesty's 90th birthday" in 1990. Designed by Giusseppe Lund with sculpture by David Wynne, they were opened by Her Majesty the Queen in July 1993. On the opposite side of the roadway is the statue of George, Lord Byron, with his faithful dog, Boatswain, lying at his feet. The statue, the work of Charles Belt, rests on a plinth of pink granite which was the gift of the Greek government.

Designed by Richard Westmacott and made from canons captured on Wellington's campaigns, the Achilles statue stands proud at the top of a hillock near to the Queen Elizabeth's gate. Its nudity caused it to be condemned by a number of persons, including William Wilberforce, the great campaigner against slavery and a "self-appointed guardian of the public's morals". Fig leaves have come and gone over the years since 1822. One irate reader of the Morning Herald wrote, *"If my mother had caught any of her children looking at such an object she would have whipped them."*

The road running parallel is Park Lane which forms part of the one-way system to and from Hyde Park Corner to Marble Arch and Oxford Street. Here are some of London's most famous hotels – the London Hilton, the Dorchester and the Grosvenor House. Behind the hotels lies Mayfair. Further along the roadway, on the left, is the Joy of Life fountain by Thomas Huxley-Jones which was unveiled in 1963. It was a gift to London by the Sigismund Goetz Fund. The bus stops at the end of Park Lane opposite Marble Arch, with **Speakers' Corner** on the left. From the eighteenth century this spot has been a popular meeting place for Londoners. In earlier days they came in droves to witness the executions that took place on the dreaded Tyburn Tree. The "Tree" stood 3 metres (11ft) high, was triangular in shape, with each side being 2.4 metres (8ft) long. Thus, it was possible to hang, draw and quarter twenty-four persons at any one time. In the twentieth century crowds still gather here, particularly at week-ends, to listen, to heckle, to interrupt the speakers. Anarchists, evangelists, anyone who wants to say something brings a box and stands to hold forth on their pet subject. Marble Arch was designed as a ceremonial entrance to Buckingham Palace in 1828 by John Nash. It is a copy of the Emperor Constantine's arch in Rome. Since it was moved here in 1851 it has been adapted to become a police station when necessary. This grew out of the fact that in the last century there were a number of riotous gatherings in the park. The Arch is also a memorial to Horatio, Lord Nelson.

After passing round the road island on which Marble Arch stands, the bus enters Edgware Road. At the end of the road on a small island is a round stone commemorating the site of the Tyburn Tree. Edgware Road runs straight for as far as the eye can see. It is the Roman Watling Street that links Dubris (Dover) – Cantiacorium (Canterbury) – Londinium (London) – Verulamium (St Albans) – Viroconium Cornoviorum (Wroxeter) and Deva (Chester). Immediately, by the bus stop, is Connaught Place. Lord Randolph Churchill, the father of Sir Winston Churchill, lived here. A blue-plaque on the wall records the fact. What it does not record is that this house was one of the first private houses to be lit by electricity in 1883.

Also close at hand is the Victory Club, a residential and social club for men and women of the armed forces. The main entrance is just around the corner in Seymour Street.

Just past Sussex Gardens, on the left, is Star Street. On the corner, standing in the window of Lloyds Bank, is a stone that marks the distance from Tyburn Gate. Passing the end of Praed Street, with The Metropole, the largest hotel in London on the corner – the bus passes under the Marylebone Flyover. Opened in October 1967, it connects the Harrow and Marylebone Roads and eases the flow of the traffic in the Edgware Road over which it passes. On the other side of the flyover is the Paddington Green Police Station, the most secure in the London area. It is the successor of the Harrow Road Police Station that was made famous in the film "The Blue Lamp" starring the late Jack Warner. The film was so popular that a television series developed out of it.

From here the route lies straight ahead, passing, on the right,

Church Street with its market open from 9am to 5pm, Tuesdays to Saturdays. Here can be bought general household items and food produce, antiques, bric-a-brac and furniture. Originally founded as the Portman Market in the early nineteenth century, it served the railway goods yard of Lisson Grove. It soon became a rival of the market at Covent Garden. Unfortunately its popularity didn't last and with the opening of Marylebone Station with its hotel in 1906, the site was sold. Church Street then took over and became the market for the area, and has remained as such ever since. Gone too is The Theatre Royal, Marylebone, on the south side of Church Street, after being bombed in the last war. The last relic of its existence disappeared in 1962 when it made way for the housing development of the street at that time.

As the Edgware Road crosses Church Street, a quick glimpse is caught of the eighteenth century St Mary's, Paddington Green Church to the left. Sarah Siddons, the eighteenth century actress, and Benjamin Robert Hayden, who committed suicide in Burwood Place, are buried here. Shortly after the tall-rise flats on the left, the roadway crosses the Regent Canal. Formed in 1812, the Regent Canal Company cut a new waterway to join the very busy Grand Junction and so link the River Thames through England to Birmingham. Today most of the traffic on the canal is made up of pleasure craft. Every year in early May a great gathering of long and narrow boats converges at Little Venice for a most spectacular event. Boats come from all over the country, and the whole area takes on a festival atmosphere.

St John's Wood Road, on the right, leads to **Lord's Cricket Ground**, the Mecca for the cricket world, and the home of the Marylebone Cricket Club (MCC). The club was founded in 1787 by Thomas Lord in Dorset Square with a match between the players of Middlesex and Essex. The MCC is now accepted as being the definitive authority on cricket throughout the world. From here to the end of the journey the roadway presents several images of the housing developments of this part of London. On one side there are the detached and semi-detached houses of the last century, and on the other the high-rise flats of more recent times. Sandwiched between and amongst them are the luxury flats of a past golden age. Alight from the bus opposite the entrance to Kilburn Park (British Rail) station and cross the roadway. Walk along Belsize Road with its small, back street shops until you reach Priory Road on the left.

Priory Road, recalling the former Kilburn Priory, reflects a fairly well-to-do suburb of the nineteenth and early twentieth centuries. The road is lined with elegant semi-detached houses and leads to Abbey Road, on the corner of which stands the parish church of **St Mary with All Souls**. Built between 1856 and 1862 to the designs of Frederick John and Horace Francis, it stands on the site of the former Kilburn Nunnery. It is built in the style of the fourteenth century (Middle Gothic) with only a portion of an ornamental brass of the head of a prioress from its past. In the early 1860s the church was "one of the leading ritualistic churches in London". It became the setting for a number of protest gatherings from persons who disagreed with the fundamentals of the Oxford Movement for the restoration of the Church of England as "the one true Catholic and Apostolic Church" in this country. In more recent years the shrine of Our Lady of Kilburn has been restored and attracts many pilgrims and others to it. The notice board tells how, in times past, the church was known as St Mary-in-the-Fields. It goes on to say that the present church was built to seat one thousand and twenty persons and cost nine thousand pounds that was raised by a nationwide "One million penny stamp donations". During the time that he was studying to become an architect, Thomas Hardy, poet and the author of "Far from the Madding Crowd", "Jude the Obscure" and other Wessex novels, lived in Kilburn and worshipped in this church. Opposite the church is Abbey Road, another reminder of the monastic origins of the neighbourhood. Cross the road and walk away from the church.

At the next road junction is Quex Road. On the corner is the newly rebuilt Church of England Primary School of St Mary's Kilburn. It is a pleasing example of modern architecture. Further along the road is the Roman Catholic Church of the Sacred Heart of Jesus designed by Augustus Welby Pugin and his son Edward Welby Pugin. It is the London home of the Order of the Oblates of Mary Immaculate. Opposite the church is Conway House which is run by the Irish Church Hostels' company. At the end of the road is Kilburn High Road with its wide variety of shops to tempt the residents and visitors alike. Stay awhile and explore them and taste their wares. The Cock public house proudly proclaims the fact that it was first licensed in 1486 and rebuilt in 1900. As befits a main route in and out of London there were, and still are, a number of hostelries in which to refresh oneself before making the return journey down the Edgware Road.

Kilburn: key to map

- **A** Parish church of St Mary with All Souls
- **B** St Mary Church of England Primary School
- **C** Catholic Church of the Sacred Heart of Jesus

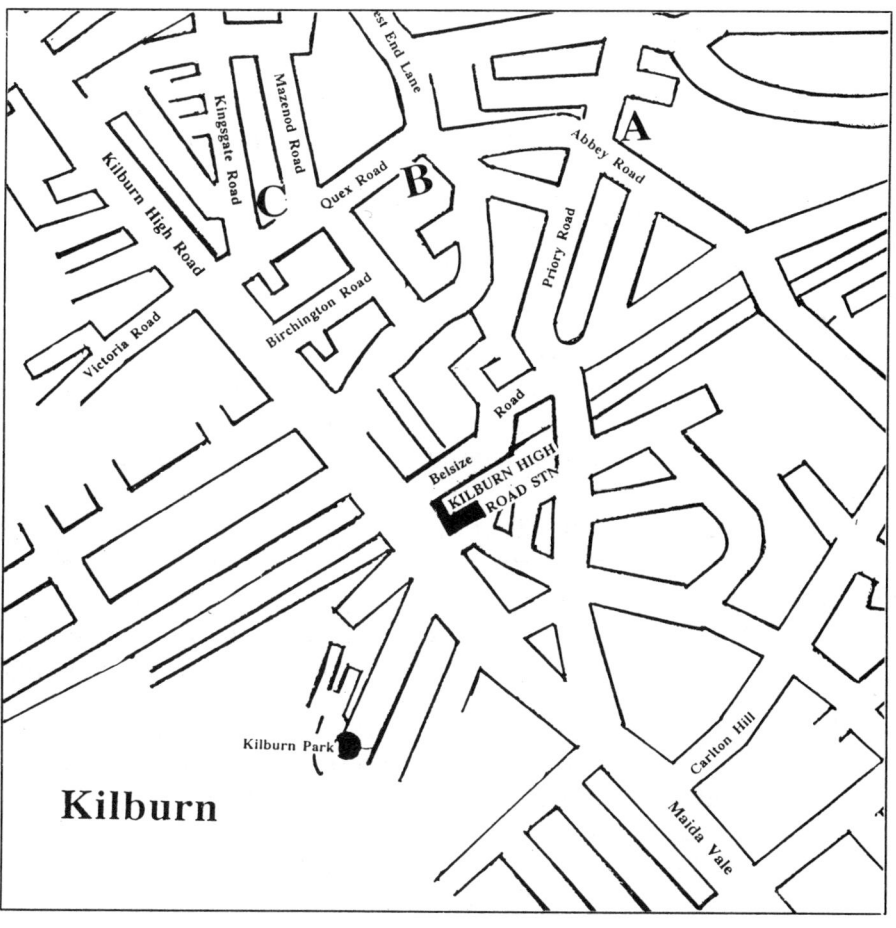

Bus Route 24: Victoria to Hampstead Heath

Route Victoria Station – Wilton Road – Victoria Street – Parliament Square – Parliament Street – Whitehall – Trafalgar Square – Charing Cross Road – Tottenham Court Road – Hampstead Road – Camden High Street – Chalk Farm Road – Ferdinand Street – Malden Road – Fleet Road – South End Green.

Start Wilton Road side of Victoria British Rail station. N.B. This service is operated by the Grey Green Company on behalf of London Transport. They use their own colours, i.e. grey and green, on their vehicles. There is a notice stating that they accept London Transport tickets.

Finish Hampstead, South End Green.

Time Allow forty to forty-five minutes for the journey.

Bus No. No. 24. The route is serviced by the Grey Green Company.

Return Either by the No. 24 bus, or British Rail train from Hampstead Heath station, South End Green. If visiting Kenwood House a 210 single-decker bus to Highgate and to Archway stops at Archway underground station (Northern Line) to return to central London.

Tickets Travelcard covering Zones 1 to 3.

A bus stop in Wilton Road, at the side of Victoria Station, is the starting point for this tour. This route is run by the Grey Green coach firm, but all London Transport tickets are valid for use on this journey.

Shortly after leaving the bus stop, on the right is the **"Apollo Victoria Theatre"** whose current production "Starlight Express" is in its third generation. The theatre was opened in 1929 and was one of the first of its kind in England to be influenced by the new Continental style that was begun in Germany by a group called the Bauhaus. After leaving Victoria Station behind, on the left ahead can be seen **"The Victoria Palace Theatre"**, opened in November 1911 as a palace of varieties or a music hall. During its early days it managed to avoid becoming another theatre for musical productions, but in the late 1920s it succumbed and Gracie Fields opened in her husband's (Archie Pitt) "The Show's the Thing". It has long been associated with light entertainment. Among its many successes was the ever-popular "Me and My Girl" in 1937, to be followed by the Crazy Gang Shows in the late 1940s. On the island in front of the theatre is Little Ben, a 10 metre (30 ft) version of St Stephen's Clock tower that stands at one end of the Houses of Parliament.

The bus moves round the one-way system and enters Bressenden Place. Here a quick look to the left reveals the statue of a rampant stag. From 1641 to the redevelopment of the site in 1959 this was the site of the Stag Brewery. Flats and offices have now replaced the buildings of the brewery. The aluminium statue was the work of E. Bainbridge and was erected here in 1962. Victoria Street lies ahead with **Westminster (Catholic) Cathedral** on the right, its piazza a gathering point for visitors and beggars alike. The cathedral is dedicated to the Precious Blood of Our Lord Jesus Christ, and was the first purpose built Catholic Cathedral in England since the Reformation of the sixteenth century. Work was begun on its construction in 1895 with the laying of the foundation stone by Cardinal Vaughan. The building was completed in 1903, but the interior is still incomplete. In the summer months a lift takes visitors high above the cathedral building, from where there are spectacular views over London. But choose a fine, clear day!

Originally The Army & Navy, Victoria, the shop on the right was a co-operative formed, in 1871, by a group of officers from the armed forces of England. Its customers were all members of either of these two branches of the Forces and their families. Within four years they had acquired sufficient funds to start their own factories. After the First World War they opened their store, for the first time, to the general public. Alas, the original intention of selling goods at a discount has long since disappeared.

On an opposite corner to the store is The Albert public house, which has an excellent reputation for good food and drink. In more leisured times they served large English breakfasts here. On the walls of the first floor restaurant can be seen portraits of two of England's greatest statesmen – Disraeli and Gladstone. An open

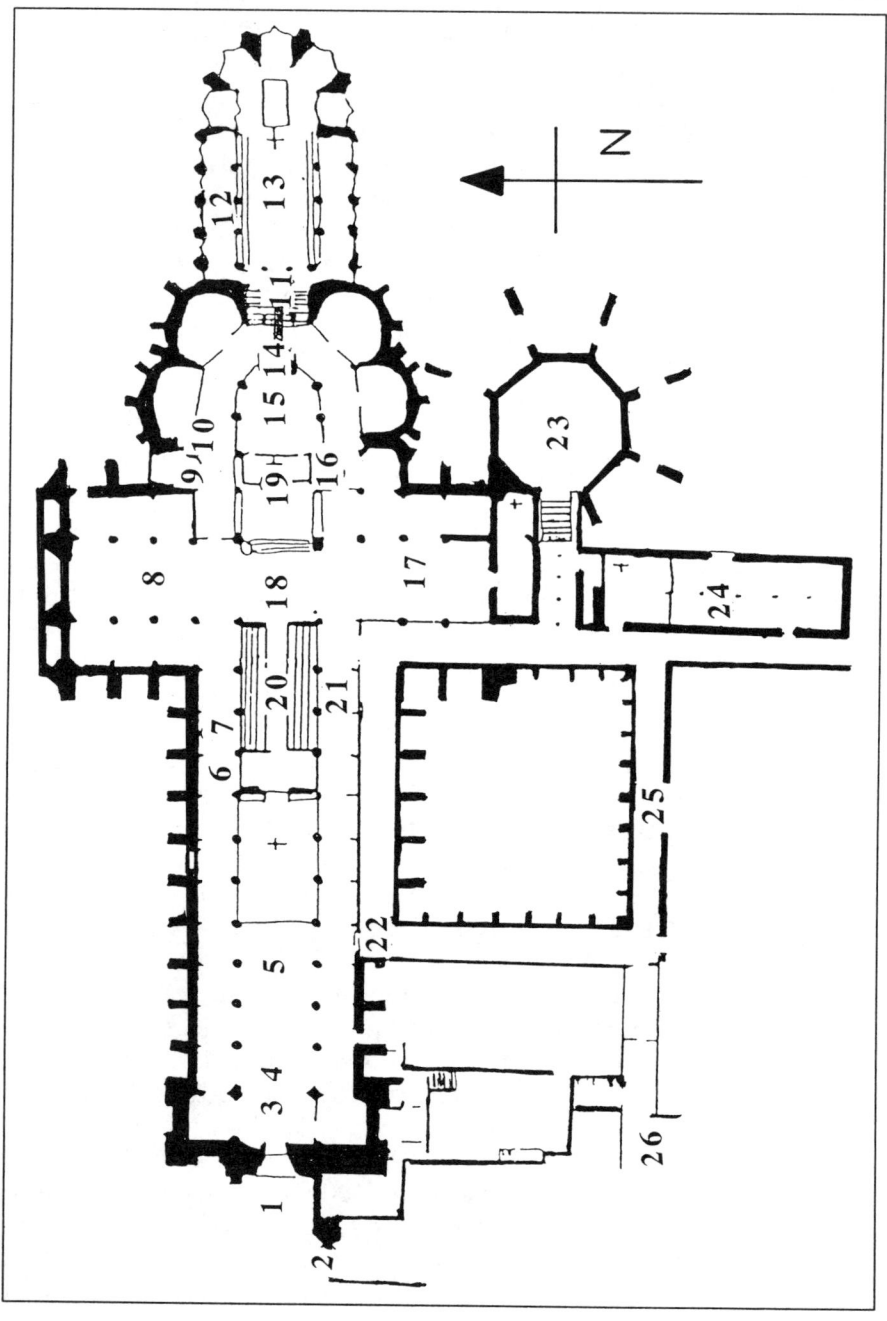

space just past the public house marks the spot where the parish church of Christ Church once stood. This was the successor to the Old Broadway Chapel that was erected here in the seventeenth century. Traditionally, its graveyard was the burial place of Captain Blood, the Irish adventurer who attempted to steal the crown jewels from the Tower of London in 1671. He was caught while trying to escape and was imprisoned in the Tower, but was pardoned by Charles II, and died in 1681.

Since 1967 the modern office block on the left has been the home of the Metropolitan Police – New Scotland Yard. Founded in 1829 in Scotland Yard off Whitehall by Sir Robert Peel, the "Met" has always kept the title wherever it has moved office. This site is the third such Scotland Yard. Anyone dialling 999 in London and asking for the police is automatically connected to the emergency room here at "The Yard".

Victoria Street was largely built in the 1850s and 1860s, although not finally completed until the 1890s. Such is the way of road building. It stretches from Westminster Abbey to Victoria Station and is a direct route between the two places. At one end of the street stands **Westminster Abbey** whose history dates back to Saxon times. Many books have been written about the Abbey, its history and associations. Come back another time and explore it yourself or join one of the conducted tours organised by the Abbey staff.

Key to plan of Westminster Abbey

1. **West front** The entrance to the Abbey is by way of the Great West Doorway. Before entering, spare a little time to look up at the building – now so pristinely clean.
2. **Bookshop** To the right of the West Door is the Abbey's bookshop. In addition to books the shop sells souvenirs, etc.
3. **Churchill memorial stone** Here is the memorial stone to one of the greatest Englishmen ever to live. He is not buried here, but at Bladon, Warwickshire.
4. **Unknown soldier's grave** Here lies buried with all due honour one of the many thousands of English soldiers who died for King and Country during the First World War, 1914-1918.
5. **Nave** Here can be seen the graves of the famous and the not so famous.

David Livingstone, the Scottish missionary, is next to Tompion the clockmaker.

6 **Ticket Office** Entrance to the area beyond the choir screen is by ticket only. Just past the desk is ...

7 **Musicians' aisle** The North Choir Aisle contains the graves or memorials of Musicians, many of whom have contributed to the music of the Abbey Choir.

8 **North transept** This transept is devoted to the men of Parliament and is known as the Politicians Corner. Burials include William Pitt, William Gladstone and William Wilberforce.

9 **Abbot Islip's chapel** The last Abbot of Westminster, Abbot Islip was responsible for the building of Henry VII's chapel. He also added the Jericho Chamber to the Abbot's house, and the Abbot's pew in the south wall of the church – now overlooking the Unknown Warrior's Tomb.

10 **"Our Lady of the Pew"** At the entrance to the former Chapel of St John the Baptist is an alabaster statue of Our Lady and the Christ Child. It was placed here in 1971 and was carved by Sister Concordia of the Order of St Benedict of Minster Abbey, Isle of Thanet, Kent – a Roman Catholic Order of nuns.

11 **Entrance to chapel** Here are the steps that lead into Henry VII's Chapel. But first turn to the left and enter the aisle in which can be seen...

12 **Elizabeth I's tomb** The Tudor Queen lies buried here, together with her half sister Mary Tudor.

13 **Henry VII's chapel** The main chapel in the Chapel of the Order of the Bath – the members' banners hang over the stalls. Within the chapel lie buried Henry VII and his wife, Elizabeth of York. The East Window, is by Hugh Easton.

14 **Henry V's Tomb** "Lancastrian king and conqueror of France." His greatest battle was in 1415 at Agincourt.

15 **Edward the Confessor's shrine** The shrine to England's saintly king is still visited every year by hundreds of pilgrims. Here in this chapel is kept the Coronation Chair.

16 **Sigbert's tomb** In a recess can be seen the tomb of Sigbert, king, and possibly founder of the Abbey.

17 **Poets' Corner** This corner of the Abbey is devoted to poets and men of literature Many are buried here, others are commemorated in stone memorials or floor slabs.

18 **Crossing** This area is known as the Coronation Theatre, for here every

monarch of England has been crowned since the time of William the Conqueror in 1066, except for Edward V and Edward VIII, the two uncrowned kings.

19 High altar The medieval stone screen has a reredos by Sir Gilbert Scott of the "Last Supper". Under the carpet the floor is covered by a mosaic brought from Rome and was, possibly. a gift from Pope Clement IV.

20 Choir stalls Erected in 1848 to the designs of Edward Blore, they replaced the ones used by the monks of medieval times. Here today the Abbey choir sings where monks once gathered eight times a day to sing their Offices (Services).

21 South choir aisle Here is the grave of Dame Sybil Thorndike, the actress, and a memorial to the Wesley Brothers, John and Charles. The doorway on the left leads into the cloisters.

22 Doorway to cloisters This is the doorway through which the monks would have entered the church during the day to attend their services. Here in the cloisters it is possible, for a small fee, to make a "rubbing" from one or more of the replica monumental brasses that can be seen in many of the parish churches throughout England.

23 Chapter House Here, daily, in medieval times the monks would gather for a Business of the Abbey meeting. After the Dissolution of the Monasteries Act of 1539, the building was bought by Parliament to store its records.

24 Undercroft museum Here are some of the earliest wax effigies to survive. For hundreds of years it was the custom at funeral processions to have a life-like figure of the deceased lying on top of the coffin. These are reminders of this ancient practice.

25 Cloisters – south walk Under the stone seats can be seen the tombs of eight of the Norman abbots of Westminster. They include Abbots Laurence, Gilbert Crispin and William de Humez.

26 Archway to Dean's Yard The Yard once formed part of the Abbey's gardens, but today houses the Westminster (Public) School, the Choir School, and the main entrance to Church House, the home of the General Synod of the Church of England.

In front of the Abbey stands a red granite column surmounted by a statue of St George and the dragon. Designed by George Gilbert Scott, it commemorates the old boys of Westminster School who were killed in the Crimean War and the Indian Mutiny. On the opposite side of the roadway, on the left, are the Queen Elizabeth II Conference Centre and the Methodist Central Hall. The former was opened by Her Majesty the Queen in 1986, and the latter was built between

1905 and 1911. The Hall stands on the site of the Royal Aquarium that was built as a place of entertainment in 1876, but was not a success and was finally demolished in 1906. Its theatre was the last part to survive; the palm trees, sculpture and aquarium with its exotic fishes having been the first to go.

Parliament Square is surrounded by buildings of great historical and architectural interest. Immediately on the corner is the former Middlesex Guildhall. The present building was designed by J.S. Gibson and the foundation stone was laid by the Duke of Westminster in May 1912. The carvings over the main entrance to the building show Hampton Court's Great Hall, and King John signing Magna Carta. They are reminders of the part that Westminster, when it formed part of the former county of Middlesex, played in the history of England. From the square the route leads into Parliament Street where there is little left of the eighteenth century buildings that once graced it. It was in 1750 that the street first appeared in the Rates Book of the City of Westminster. Only numbers 43 and 44, on the right, remain today, the rest have been redeveloped. In the nineteenth century the roadway was widened as part of a general improvement to the approach to the new Westminster Bridge. New government offices were also built. The street is the widest in London at 43 metres wide (130ft).

Whitehall: key to map

1. **War Cabinet rooms** Billed as being the "Nerve Centre of Britain's war effort" between August 1939 and August 1945, these underground rooms, some twenty- one in number, became the every day work place of the Prime Minister. Now they are open for inspection by the general public. There is an admission charge.
2. **Cenotaph** Originally made of plasterboard as part of the Peace Celebration after the First World War (1914-1918), it captured the imagination of the British Nation and was rebuilt in Portland Stone. It was designed by Sir Edwin Lutyens, the consultant and architect for the Imperial War Graves Commission. Here the annual Armistice Ceremony takes place every November.
3. **No. 10 Downing Street** The official London residence of the First Lord of the Treasury – the Prime Minister. In the late seventeenth century Sir George Downing built a cul-de-sac of twenty four plain, brick, terraced houses. All that remain are Numbers 10, 11 and 12.

Bus Route 24: Victoria to Hampstead Heath

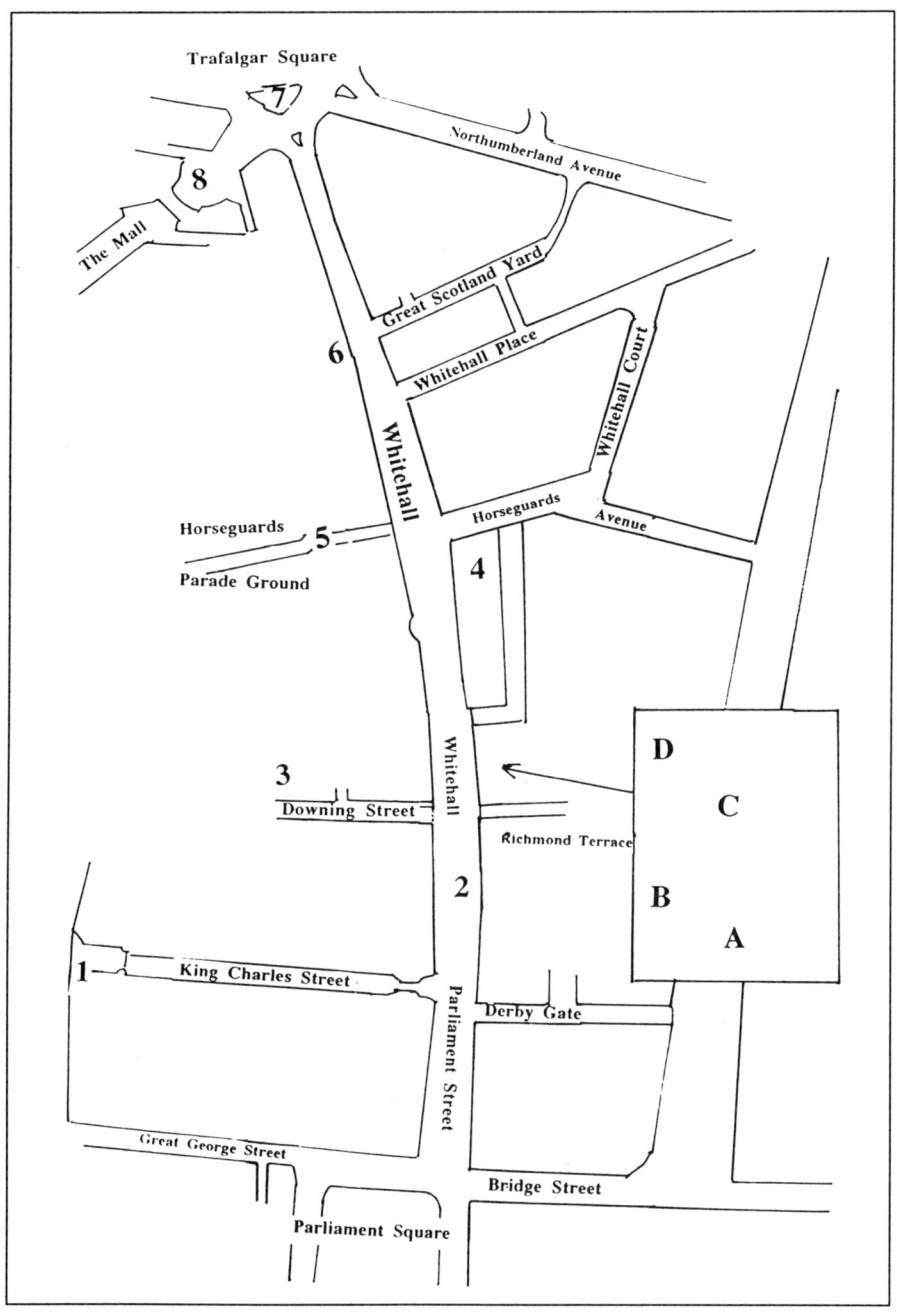

4   **Banqueting House** The only remaining part of the last Whitehall Palace above ground. The work of Inigo Jones for James I after fire had destroyed its predecessor.

5   **Horse Guards** Originally a small guard house built on the side of the Tiltyard of Whitehall Palace. Replaced in 1665 by a building to accommodate the King's Guards. The present group of buildings were designed by William Kent between 1750 and 1758. Only members of the Royal Family are permitted to drive through the central archway.

6   **Admiralty House** Originally the official residence of the First Lord of the Admiralty and built to a design of Samuel Pepys Cockerill, it is joined to the former Admiralty Office. The functions of the latter are now catered for at the Ministry of Defence building in Horse Guards Avenue. The screen and entrance to the courtyard was the work of Robert Adam in the eighteenth century.

7   **Statue of Charles I** This contemporary statue of Charles I was commissioned by Lord Weston, Lord High Treasurer of England in 1631. The date of its completion, 1633, is moulded on the under part of the right foot of the horse. It was the work of Hubert Le Sueur. That it survived the Commonwealth can only be described as miraculous.

8   **The Mall** The finest processional way in Europe, leading as it does to Buckingham Palace. It was created as part of the improvements to St James's Park and the surrounding area at the time of the Restoration of the monarchy of the 1660s.

The national memorial to the Glorious Dead of two World Wars, the Cenotaph, stands in the centre of the roadway. Designed by Sir Edwin Lutyens and originally made of plasterboard, it so captured the imagination of the general public that this permanent structure was commissioned and built. A pair of fine wrought iron gates guard the end of Downing Street where Number 10 is the home, during his or her term of office, of the Prime Minister of Great Britain. Sir George Downing, soldier and diplomat, was born in Ireland about 1623, and in 1638 emigrated with his parents to New England where he founded Harvard College. He returned to England during the time of the Civil War when he fought on the side of the Parliamentarians against the King's Army. At the Restoration of the monarchy in 1660 he continued to serve England and, for "services rendered", was given a plot of land here. He developed the site for twenty-four houses, of which only three remain today. It is interesting to note that Number 10 was once the site of the Cockpit (theatre) of Whitehall Palace.

On the right-hand side of the roadway are the statues of:

A. Field Marshal, The Viscount Montgomery of Alamein. The English soldier who commanded the British Forces during the North Africa campaign of the Second World War. He was familiarly known as "Monty".

B. Field Marshal, The Viscount Alanbrook. Soldier and master of strategy in World War II, he was in command of the 2nd Corps at the time of the retreat from Dunkirk, and later became the Chief of the Imperial General Staff.

C. Sir Walter Raleigh. English courtier, navigator, and poet at the time of Elizabeth I. He successfully introduced tobacco and potatoes into Britain.

D. Field Marshal, The Viscount Slim. English soldier who fought in the First World War. In 1943 he was appointed Commander of 14th 'forgotten' army in Burma which he led to victory in 1945. He spent the latter part of his life as Governor General of Australia.

Just past the statues is **The Banqueting House,** the only remaining complete building of the former Whitehall Palace, the rest having been destroyed by fire in the late seventeenth century. Opposite stands **Horse Guards** with the mounted guards on duty. The changing of the Guard each morning during the summer is a strong attraction for both visitors and Londoners alike. At the head of Whitehall stands the equestrian statue of Charles I of England by Hubert Le Sueur, with a pedestal designed by Christopher Wren and carved by Grinling Gibbons. The date 1632 appears on the foot of the horse. Every year on the anniversary of the King's execution a short service of prayer is said here after which various royalist societies lay wreaths. On the Sunday nearest the 30th of January, the "King's Army", part of the English Civil War Society, re-enacts the king's last walk from St James's Palace to Whitehall. Wreaths are laid both at the Banqueting House and at the foot of the statue at the head of Whitehall.

Further along the street on the left is the former Admiralty House. Built between 1722 and 1726, it was designed by Thomas Ripley, with Robert Adam adding the front stone screen in 1761. Since 1964 the Ministry of Defence, established during the last War to co-ordinate the work of the three armed forces, has been housed in its own building behind the Banqueting House. Leaving Whitehall, the bus passes **Admiralty Arch** on the left, through which can be seen Buckingham Palace at the far end of The Mall. The arch was built in 1910, designed by Sir Aston Webb, and was part of a national memorial to Queen Victoria. Bus stop C in Trafalgar Square is in front of the National Gallery and offers the bus passenger a chance to survey the square. From here can be seen the 48 metre (145ft) column with the statue of Horatio, Lord Nelson, the victor of the sea battle of Trafalgar on the top.

At the parish church of St Martin-in-the-Fields, the bus turns left into Charing Cross Road where, almost immediately, on the right, is the statue to Nurse Edith Cavell. She was executed in Brussels on 12th October 1915 after being found guilty of conspiring to help British soldiers escape from occupied enemy territory. Her last words are recorded on the plinth, "Patriotism is not enough. I must have no hatred or bitterness for anyone." She lies buried outside the east end of Norwich Cathedral. Opposite the statue, on the left, is **The National Portrait Gallery** which was founded in 1856 at the suggestion of the 5th Earl of Stanhope. It now houses some 8,000 portraits. Not all are on permanent display on the walls, but on request pictures from the reserve stock can be made available. "It is a research institute on British historical portraiture as well as a panorama of British history."

On the next corner, just beyond the Gallery, is a statue of Sir Henry Irving, the eighteenth century actor. His acting in Shakespearean plays, both in this country and America, is legendary in theatrical circles. He was knighted in 1895 when he became the First Knight of the Theatre. Another great hero of the English stage, David Garrick, is remembered in **"The Garrick Theatre"** on the right. It was built in 1889 and designed by Walter Emden and C.J. Phipps, leading theatrical architects of the nineteenth century. There is a copy of Gainsborough's portrait of Garrick hanging in the foyer. **"Wyndhams Theatre"**, on the right, was built by Charles Wyndham, designed by W.G.R. Sprague, and opened in November 1899 with a revival of T.W. Robertson's "David Garrick". Raymond Mander and Joe Mitchenson, in their book "The Theatres of London", record, *"The theatre opened on 16 November 1899 with a revival of David Garrick, and on this occasion Wyndham handed over the total re-*

ceipts, £4,000, to the Aldershot Branch of the Soldiers' Wives and Families Association. This magnanimous gesture was widely supported..."

Cambridge Circus, named after the Duke of Cambridge who "opened" Charing Cross Road in 1887, is the point where the road crosses Shaftesbury Avenue. "The Palace Theatre" opened as the Royal English Opera House in January 1891 with "Ivanhoe" by Arthur Sullivan. Its life as a centre of English Opera was short-lived, and in the following year it became a Palace of Variety – a music hall. Over the last few decades it has been the home of a number of highly successful musical productions. Long may they continue to entertain us! Before reaching the end of this road, on the right, is **"The Phoenix Theatre"**, one of London's 1930s buildings. Sir Giles Gilbert Scott was the architect of the building with Thomas Komisarjevsky being responsible for the interior. Scott's other works include Waterloo Bridge, the red telephone boxes, and the Anglican Cathedral in Liverpool – a man of diverse architectural abilities.

Towering over London's skyline and Charing Cross Road in particular is Centre Point. Built during the office building boom of the 1960s, it was completed in 1971, and remained empty for a number of years. Today it is the headquarters of the Confederation of British Industry (CBI) which represents the interests of British business. Tottenham Court Road lies ahead with "The Dominion Theatre" on the right. Built in 1929, it stands on part of the site that was once occupied by Meux's Horse Shoe Brewery. The brewery's claim for recognition in the history of London dates back to 1809. A vat standing seven metres (22ft) high, and containing sufficient Porter – a dark sweet ale brewed from black malt – to fill nearly four thousand barrels burst. The result played havoc with the members of the local community, and eight lives were lost. They were all buried in a portery grave! On the corner of Great Russell Street stands the Young Men's Christian Association (YMCA) which was founded in 1843 by a young draper's assistant named George Williams. At the first meeting the object was declared as being *"the improvement of the spiritual condition of young men and mental culture."* From that meeting, held in George Williams's bedroom near to Blackfriars, the present day worldwide organisation had its beginnings. Shortly afterwards he also founded the Young Women's Christian Association (YWCA). It, too, still flourishes and its building can be seen in Great Russell Street, not far from the YMCA.

Further along the road on the left is the American Church – "a church for all people". The original church (Tabernacle) was built in 1756 for George Whitefield, the Methodist preacher at whose funeral in 1770 John Wesley preached. Whitefield built his own place of worship here after being told never to preach in St Martin-in-the-Fields again. Severely damaged in the Second World War when a rocket bomb fell on it, it was later rebuilt and became the American Church in London.

At the next major cross-roads, Tottenham Court Road passes over the Euston Road underpass while the bus continues its journey along Hampstead Road. On the corner on the left are the offices and studios of Capital Radio, one of the commercial radio stations of London. Where the road joins Camden High Street, on the right is Mornington Crescent underground station. Opposite the station is the statue of Richard Cobden, the Apostle of Free Trade. The list of subscribers to the cost of the statue was headed by Napoleon III. It was a token of gratitude from the Emperor for his services in negotiating a trade tariff agreement with France. He was also a strong pacifist and lost his seat in Parliament over being opposed to the Crimean War. During the time of the American Civil War he played a leading role in easing the tensions between the Lincoln administration and Palmerston government in England. Cobden was the father-in-law of W.R. Sickert, the German-born British artist who founded the Camden Town Group of artists in 1910.

Camden High Street is a typical high street shopping centre with shops, large and small, offering a wide range of products to locals and visitors alike. At the end of the street the roadway becomes Chalk Farm Road, recalling a farm that was notorious as being the centre for duellists. Here there is a street market in Inverness Street and another, mainly arts and crafts, open air market at Camden Lock. The latter is located to the left just before the railway bridge over Chalk Farm Road. Camden Lock is part of the Regent Canal that leads in one direction to the Limehouse Dock on the banks of the River Thames, and in the other to Little Venice. It is possible to take trips on the canal from this point.

At Ferdinand Street the bus turns right and journeys along to Malden Road, passing on its way housing estates, flats and terraced houses. At the end of the roadway in Southampton Road is the Roman Catholic Dominican Priory with its school close by. The foundation stone of the Priory Church of Our Lady of the Rosary and St Dominic was laid in 1863, in the presence of Cardinal Wiseman, the first Roman Catholic Archbishop of Westminster. However, building work did not make much progress until 1874 as the original foundations of the church were considered inadequate to support the proposed church. A fresh start had to be made to correct this serious fault. The church was opened for services in 1883, and finally consecrated in 1923 by Cardinal Bourne, the fourth Cardinal Archbishop of Westminster.

Southampton Road leads to Fleet Road (a reminder that the River Fleet rises in the Kenwood and Hampstead Ponds) and finally to South End, the finishing point for the journey. In Pond Street, off South End, is the Royal Free Hospital, founded in 1828 by William Marsden. As a young surgeon he had found a dying woman on the steps of St Andrew's Church, Holborn. She had been unable to find a subscriber to recommend her for hospital treatment. At that time there were few, if any, hospitals that offered a free service to patients. So the Royal Free Hospital was born, with George IV as its royal patron. The first patient to this present building was admitted in 1974 when the original buildings in Grays Inn Road were closed. A short walk from the bus stop is Hampstead Heath – with Kenwood and Parliament Fields it totals some 320 hectares (800 acres).

Off East Heath Road is Keats Grove where **Keats House** and library are well worth a visit. Here are two lovely semi-detached cottages, now made into one house. John Keats spent a large portion of his working life here. While sitting in the garden he wrote "Ode to a Nightingale", and "Endymion" (1818), and in the following year he wrote his great odes – "On a Grecian Urn" and "To Autumn", and so on. The house is open to the public for a small fee that includes an excellent recorded tour of the house and its contents. For the more energetic walker, the Heath offers a number of attractive walks, one of which leads to **Kenwood House**. The house, on the far side of the heath, was originally built in 1616, but was later largely rebuilt by Robert Adam. It contains a fine collection of paintings by such artists as Rembrandt and Vermeer, as well as furniture of the eighteenth century. The piece-de-resistance for many is Robert Adam's superbly designed library. In the summer months open-air concerts are held by the lakeside and are very popular events.

From the entrance to Kenwood House in Hampstead Lane single-decker buses return the visitor to either Golders Green Station or to Highgate and Archway station. The former route passes The Spaniards public house en route. Its origins are debated by historians. One school of thought says that it was once the home of the Spanish Ambassador, the other says it was owned by two Spanish gentlemen who ran it as a place of refreshment. The story goes that they both fell in love with the same lady. In order to decide who should be allowed to marry, they fought a duel in the courtyard of the house. The victor entered the bar to claim his prize, only to find that the lady had left with another gentleman, never to be seen again! In remorse, he went into the courtyard once more and buried his brother there. It is claimed that late at night the clashing of swords can be heard in the courtyard! "Dick" Turpin, the notorious highwayman, and his horse are also heard arriving in the dead of night! The Highgate route passes through the village with its old inns and modern eating places to attract the passenger to stop off and investigate.

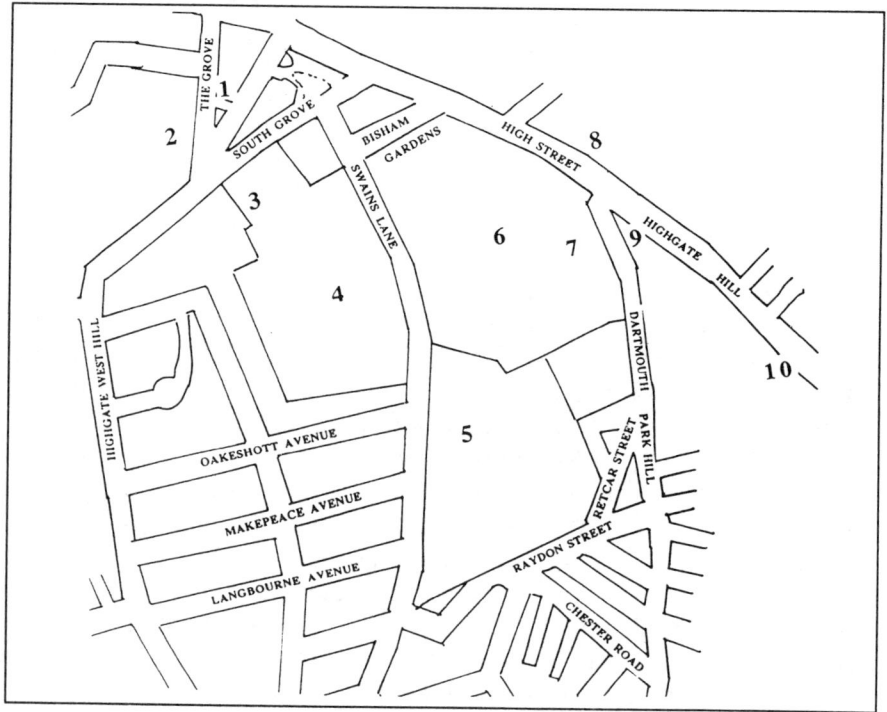

Highgate: key to map

1 **The Flask Public House** Originally a farm house at the top of the hill, the present building dates from the seventeenth century. It makes a pleasant stopping off place for a rest and drink.

2 **The Grove** A row of late seventeenth and eighteenth century houses, in one of which lived Samuel Taylor Coleridge. He is buried in the parish church of St Michael.

3 **Church of St Michael** Built on the site of Ashurst House, the home of Sir William Ashurst, Lord Mayor of London in 1694, the church was designed by Lewis Vulliamy in 1830. In the porch under the west tower is a mark indicating the top of the cross on St Paul's cathedral.

4 **Highgate Cemetery (west)** In the nineteenth century a large number of private cemeteries were laid out in the, then, suburbs, of London, partly for hygienic reasons and partly for money. Many famous persons chose to be buried in this section of the cemetery, including Charles Cruft, founder of the dog show and the wife and daughter of Charles Dickens. More recent burials include Jacob Bronowski, scientist, and Patrick Wyman, the actor. This part of the cemetery is only open for guided tours. There is a charge.

5 **Highgate Cemetery (East)** Included in this section's burials are Karl Marx, the Communist Leader; George Eliot, the pseudonym of Mary Ann (Marian) Evans, and the authoress of "Adam Bede" and "Middlemarch", William Foyle, the founder of Foyle's Book Shop in Charing Cross Road, as well as William Friese-Green, inventor of cinematography.

6 **Waterlow Park** A gift to the people of London from Sir Sydney Waterlow, a nineteenth century Lord Mayor of London. From the upper reaches of the Park views over London can be seen on a fine, clear day.

7 **Lauderdale House** Dates from the sixteenth century but with additions in the next two centuries. It was the home of the Second Earl (later) Duke of Lauderdale. Samuel Pepys, the seventeenth century diarist, visited the house in July 1666 and recorded that he listened to a servant playing the violin.

8 **Cromwell House** Built about 1637-38 by Richard Sprignell, a captain in the London Trained (Train) bands who were the forerunners of the Militia and Territorial Forces. The house is remarkable for its cut and moulded brickwork and contains a contemporary staircase once famous for its carved figures of soldiers. They were stolen in the 1980s. There is no evidence for any connection with the Cromwell family; the house acquired the name in 1833.

9   **Church of St Joseph** The Roman Catholic Congregation of the Passion of Jesus Christ (The Passionists) work from this church. The church was designed by John Tasker, architect and builder. Some of his drawings are now held in the Library of the Royal Institute of British Architects (RIBA).

10 **Whittington's stone** Traditionally where Richard "Dick" Whittington sat and heard the bells of Saint Mary Le Bow church in the City of London telling him to turn again and become (Lord) Mayor of London. He did and he was!

After a visit to the village of Highgate, it is a short walk down Highgate Hill to Archway underground station or to a number of buses that will return the walker to central London.

Bus Route 73: Marble Arch to Stoke Newington

Route Marble Arch (Park Lane) – Oxford Street – Oxford Circus – Oxford Street – Tottenham Court Road – Euston Road – Euston Square – King's Cross – Pentonville Road – Upper Street – Islington Green – Essex Road – Newington Green – Albion Road – Stoke Newington Church Street

Start Park Lane, Hyde Park, Marble Arch end.

Finish Stoke Newington Church Street

Time Allow fifty minutes for the journey.

Bus No. 73

Return By bus 73.

Tickets To cover Zones 1 to 3.

Board the bus at the Marble Arch end of Park Lane. The destination board should read either Stoke Newington or Tottenham. The route immediately circumnavigates the island on which the Arch stands and enters Oxford Street.

Marble Arch was designed by John Nash, the favourite architect of the Prince Regent (later George IV) as a ceremonial entrance to Buckingham Palace and was intended as a memorial to Horatio, Lord Nelson. It was moved to its present position in 1851 and was used as an entrance to Hyde Park. During the re-routing of Park Lane in the 1960s, an island was constructed around it. A copy of Emperor Constantine's arch in Rome, it is made of Carrara marble and cost £100,000. The relief on the north side is by Richard Westmacott and the one on the south by E.H. Bailey (he also sculpted the figure of Nelson in Trafalgar Square). Passage through the arch is permitted only to senior members of the Royal Family and the King's Troop Royal Horse Artillery.

Most people who come to London will want to go shopping in Oxford Street. It is one of the busiest shopping streets in London, and has been a major thoroughfare since the time of the Roman occupation of Britain. It is the roadway that leads from Hampshire, South England, via London, to Suffolk, an eastern county. Both sides of the road are lined with shops to entice the tourist and the Londoner to buy. Recent improvements have included widening the pavement (side walks) and exercising a better control over the traffic that flows through the street. A slight dip in the roadway just past Selfridge's Store reflects the fact that one of London's lost rivers flows underneath the road here – the River Tyburn. When Bond Street station was being built at the end of the nineteenth century the engineers had constant problems with the river. On more than one occasion the water flooded the tunnel and the area of the station.

At the junction with Regent Street is Oxford Circus, where the bus continues across the circus to Tottenham Court Road and turns left. The street is lined with shops, many of them specialising in electronic equipment. On the right is Great Russell Street, the home of the British Museum and a number of interesting bookshops. Tottenham Court Road once led from the village of St Giles in the Fields (close to where Centre Point now stands) to the prebendal Manor of Toten or Ten Hale that is mentioned in the Domesday Survey of 1086.

Euston Road, which crosses over the end of the road, was first built in the eighteenth century – as London's first by-pass! It forms part of a roadway that led from Lancaster Gate off the Bayswater Road, to Smithfield Cattle Market, outside the City Wall. The road was to enable the cattle going to be either sold or slaughtered to avoid the West End and so allow the passenger coaches an easier ride to the City. On the right is the Wellcome Institute for the History of Medicine with its free library open to students and persons doing private research. An appointment to view may be necessary. The original library belonged to Sir Henry Wellcome, the manufacturing chemist and scientist. His collection of artefacts was transferred to the Science Museum in South Kensington in 1976 where they now form part of the two Wellcome Galleries. Just beyond the Wellcome Institute is the Friends' House, built between 1925 and 1927 to the designs of Hubert Lidbetter. It houses a large meeting room as well as offices and a library. The latter has a fine collection of literature relating to the Quaker Movement including George Fox's journal recalling the foundation of the Colony of Pennsylvania. William

Penn founded the colony that was to take his name as a Quaker Foundation. "Quakers reject such externals as Sacraments in favour of the 'inner light' of Jesus Christ in the soul. Correctly called the Society of Friends their nickname seems to have originated from the trembling that they experience at the presence of God at their meetings".

Opposite the Friends' Meeting House is Euston Square, behind which can be seen **Euston Station**. It was here, or nearby, that Richard Trevithick, "father of the locomotive", in 1808 laid out an experimental railway track – in a circular formation. The London and Birmingham Railway was the first line to reach this part of London in 1838. Bureaucrats would not allow the stations nearer to central London than the edge of the "New Road". Today Euston is the West Coast Main Line terminus and has a handsome station opened in 1968 by Her Majesty Queen Elizabeth II. Nearby can be seen the "new church" of St Pancras which was opened in 1822 and designed by the Inwoods (father and son). One of the most expensive churches built in the nineteenth century, it is based on the Erechtheion in Athens. Henry Inwood had just returned from Athens with a set of drawings and measurements when they received the commission to build the church. The Temple of the Winds forms the west tower, and the side porches are supported by terracotta caryatids modelled by Rossi.

In 1888 the Elizabeth Garrett Anderson Hospital, on the left, moved here from Marylebone Road after having been founded in 1866 in Seymour Place, off the Edgware Road. The founder, after whom the hospital was named, was the first woman in England to qualify as a doctor in 1865. It is still the only hospital in London where women are treated by women. All this in spite of various Equal Opportunities legislation.

On the left is the site for the new **British Library** which, when it is complete, will house all the books that are at the present time housed in the British Museum in Great Russell Street. The library is one of the Copyright Libraries of the United Kingdom. Copies of all books, newspapers and magazines published in this country have to be sent to these libraries by their publishers. The other five are the National Library of Wales, National Library of Scotland, Trinity College, Dublin, and the Oxford and Cambridge University Libraries. The National Newspaper Library has been housed in a special building in Colindale, North London since the 1930s. Tickets are required to use the British Library and applications should be made to the Library Admissions Office at the Museum.

In 1863 the Midland Railway Company bought a plot of land in the centre of Agar Town – a typically run-down slum area of London at that time. Here they built, to the designs of George Gilbert Scott, **St Pancras Station Hotel**. Behind the hotel, R.C. Ordish, a notable engineer and builder of railway stations, erected the station designed by W.H. Barlow. They have become one of the wonders of the nineteenth century. The station, with its great arched roof 210 metres (689ft) long and spanning 74 metres (242ft), rises 30 metres (100ft) above the rails at its apex. The two hundred and fifty bedroom hotel was described by George Augustus Sala, English journalist and novelist, as being " the most sumptuous and best conducted hotel in the Empire". The outside has recently been superbly cleaned and now looks like new.

The final station alongside the Euston Road is **King's Cross**, designed by Thomas Cubitt. It was built on the site of the London Smallpox Hospital, in a district originally known as Battle Bridge. When it was opened it was the largest railway station in England. According to some historians Battle Bridge was the site of the final battle between the Romans and the Iceni Queen Boudicea. The queen was defeated in the battle and rather then being taken prisoner, she took poison and died. Traditionally she lies buried under one of the platforms of the station. The clock in the central tower of the facade was made by Dents, the clockmakers, for the Great Exhibition of 1851 held in Hyde Park.

Pentonville Road leads away from the station towards Islington. About half way up the hill, on the left, is the former St James's Chapel, built by Aaron Hurst in 1787 as a propriety chapel on the Pentonville Estate. A propriety chapel, and there were a number of them built in the eighteenth century, were places of worship, but without the status of parish churches. They were built in areas that were away from the parish church. They were often privately built for use by those members of the parish who considered the church too far away from their homes. Pevsner describes the building as being *"very pretty Adamesque style"* with its front made of Coade Stone. Coade stone was made on the site where the Royal Festival Hall now stands on the South Bank. The secret formula for making this most weather-proof stone was lost when the last member of the Coade Family died, and in 1840 the Coade Artificial Stone Manufactory was closed. The original patent by Richard Holt expired in the 1720s and Mrs Eleanor Coade took over, but the improved formula was never patented.

In the centre of Claremont Square, on the right, is the New River Head's Upper Reservoir. The New River Company was formed in the early seventeenth century to bring fresh water by natural and artificial means to London. From springs and wells near Ware, in Hertfordshire, Sir Hugh Myddelton undertook the task to bring and supply in four years. Originally some thirty-eight miles long (but only twenty as the crow flies), today it is only twenty four miles long and terminates at the Stoke Newington Water Works, in Green Lane. Parts of the redundant stretches of the waterway have now been landscaped and make a pleasant oasis for Londoners to enjoy. The "one-way-system" from Pentonville Road leads to Islington's Upper Street where there are numerous shops and two of the most popular antiques markets in London. The first is **The Mall Antiques Arcade**, and close by is **Camden Passage**. Both are very popular markets. Islington is another of London's lost villages that has much to offer the explorer. Behind the shops is the Business Design Centre in the former Royal Agricultural Hall. It is now a place for exhibitions and conferences.

An essential for a village is a village green, and Islington has one at the junction of Essex Road and Upper Street. Here stands the statue of Hugh Myddelton, the financier behind the New River Project, by John Thomas. On the far side of the green once stood the famous Collins Music Hall. Not a Palace of Varieties as other music halls, but more a place to go to listen to songs and drink beer. It was originally The Lansdowne Arms public house but Sam Collins had problems obtaining a licence for music so he enlarged the building and turned it into a music hall with a liquor licence. It ended its life in 1956 when fire completely destroyed it. Only memories of its past are left today with a blue plaque marking the site. It was also reputed to have two ghosts, but they have not been seen or heard since the theatre was demolished. Essex Road is traditionally associated with the Earl of Essex, Robert Devereux, who is said to have been visited by Elizabeth I. The local hostelry, The Old Queen's Head, on the right, is said to have been built on the site of his house. Is the ghost that haunts the house Elizabeth I? Essex Road is a mixture of houses, shops and flats that have been built in the past two hundred years.

The road leads to Newington Green which was created in the fifteenth century out of part of the great Middlesex Forest. It wasn't until the mid-eighteenth century that the green was railed in for the first time and houses began to appear around it. It is likely that the green was used as a place of entertainment and sporting events. On the south side of the green stood Mildmay House, the home of Sir Henry Mildmay, one of the regicides who consented to the death of Charles I. After the Restoration of the Monarchy in 1660 he was tried, found guilty of treason and sentenced to life imprisonment. A warrant was issued for his transportation to Tangiers in 1664, but he died on the way. On the site of his house today is a hospital.

Albion Road leads out of the green to Stoke Newington Church Street. Alight from the bus at the request stop (press the bell once only) at the end of the road. Walk forward and turn left at the T-junction and walk along to the new (nineteenth century) parish church of **St Mary**. Built in the style of the fourteenth century by George Gilbert Scott, it was consecrated in 1858. Regarded as one of the choicest of Scott's works, it presents a lofty, handsome appearance to visitors today. If the church is locked and unattended, it is still possible to view by means of the glass panels in the inner west doorway of the church.

Across the road is the old parish church of St Mary, of which there are no early records extant. John Stow, the sixteenth century historian and antiquarian, refers to the church as being "newly builded" in 1563 (on the site of an older church) by the Lord of the Manor, William Patten. In the nineteenth century Charles Barry, architect of the Houses of Parliament, added a new north aisle to the church building.

Close by the church is **Clissold Park**, a pleasant oasis and a reminder of the countryside here many years ago. Within the park there is a children's zoo and playground as well as a nursery where children can be left and looked after by qualified staff. The eighteenth century house is now a refreshment place. The Reverend August Clissold, curate of the parish, married Miss Croatia whose father had bought the house and the land. On her father's death she inherited the lease for which the rent was one hundred and nine pounds and a fat turkey each year. After relaxing in the park, return to Church Street where, opposite the former Town Hall, there is a bus stop from where the bus will return you to Oxford Street. Alternatively, a short walk along Stoke Newington Church Street on the left-hand side will bring the walker to the Abney Park Cemetery. Here are buried, among many others, the bodies of General William Booth and his wife, founders of the Salvation Army.

Short trips to Tourist Attractions

Bus Route 11: Victoria to Chelsea

Route   Victoria Street — Buckingham Palace Road — Pimlico Road — Lower Sloane Street.
Start   Victoria Street, outside shopping arcade.
Finish Chelsea Lower Sloane Street. Request bus stop.
Time   Allow ten to fifteen minutes.
Bus No. 11
Return Reverse direction
Tickets Travelcard to cover Zone 1.

The journey starts from the bus stop in Victoria Street near to the exit from the underground station. At Buckingham Palace Road the bus turns past the entrance to Victoria railway and bus stations and **The Grosvenor Hotel** on the left. As with the Grosvenor House Hotel in Park Lane, this building stands on land owned by the Duke of Westminster and takes its name from another of his titles, Baron Grosvenor. The hotel was built in 1861 on land adjacent to Sir John Fowler's railway station of the previous year. Between 1902 and 1908, a new elaborate facade was built under the direction of Sir Charles Morgan, the chief engineer of the London, Chatham and Dover Railway Company. Both buildings are built over the dock that once was the end of the Alexandra Canal. Its lock entrance is now used by the local council as a waste disposal centre. Here the barges come and remove the city's rubbish to be taken down the river and unloaded in the North Sea.

On the corner of Elizabeth Street and Buckingham Palace Road, on the right, stands the Victoria Coach Station. Built in the early 1930s with later additions, it was designed by Wallis Gilbert & Partners. Pevsner, writing in London, volume one of his "Buildings of England" series of books, describes it as *"an impressive demonstration of the new architectural style at that time"*. It is the main, central coach station for London, from here it is possible to travel to the four corners of the United Kingdom in luxury and comfort.

At the next road junction the route passes along Pimlico Road, with the parish church, Clergy House, and Parochial School of **St**

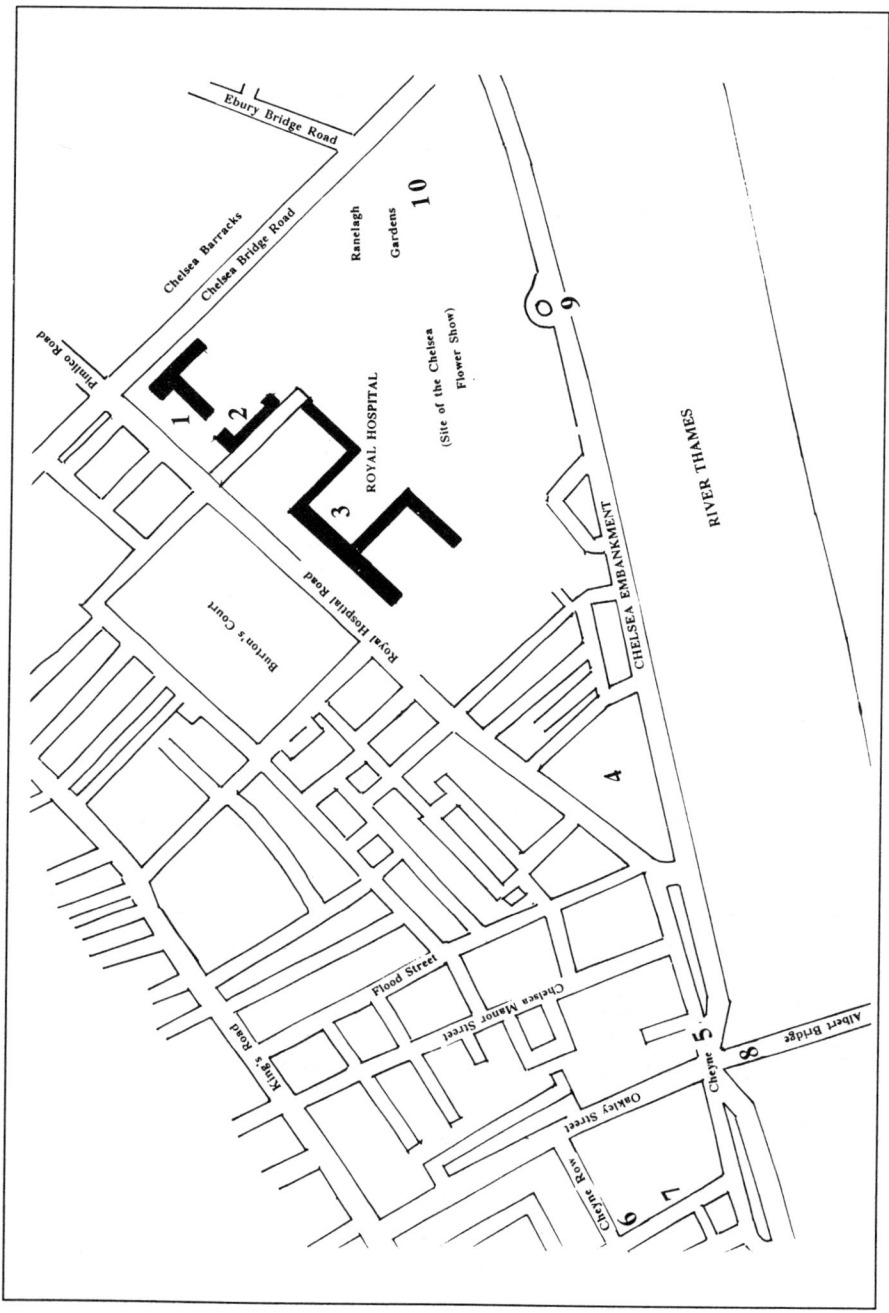

Barnabas on the corner of St Barnabas Street. All three buildings were the work of Thomas Cundy, the principal architect for the Belgravia and Pimlico estates of the Duke of Westminster. In the beginning it was the daughter church of St Paul's, Knightsbridge, for which it was built. Shortly after its completion in 1850, the church became the centre of controversy due to its liturgical practices. Matins and evensong were sung daily and there was a daily celebration of Holy Communion. Furthermore, the sexes were separated "males to the right and females to the left". It became a fashionable church to attend, and at the same time earned the title "Convent of the Belgravians".

When the Mozart family came to London in 1764, they took up residence with Dr. Sandal in Fivefields Row, Chelsea. Today that address is 180, Ebury Street, on the right, where the street meets Pimlico Road. Mozart came to London to play before George III and Queen Charlotte. It was while staying here that he wrote his first symphony. Mozart was eight years old at the time, his elder sister Marianne, eleven, helped him with the copying. A brown commemorative plaque marks the house today. On the left at the end of the road are the **Chelsea Barracks**. Built originally in 1861 for one thousand foot soldiers of the British Army, they were completely rebuilt in 1960-1961. Here the bus turns right into Lower Sloane Street. Alight from the bus at the nearest stop to visit the area.

Chelsea: key to map

1. **Burial Ground** Between 1691 and 1855 this plot of land was used as the hospital's burial ground. Some 10,000 pensioners and others persons connected with the hospital are buried here. There are "two strangers" buried here. Two women who joined the Army in search of husbands and whose presence was not discovered until they were wounded in the Crimean War. The **Infirmary** was opened in 1961 and replaces the one destroyed in the last War.

2. **Museum** Just inside the London Gate entrance to The Royal Hospital is the Wellington Hall and Museum building. All items in the collection have a direct link with the hospital and its inmates. In the Wellington Hall can be seen George Jones's gigantic painting of the Battle of Waterloo.

3. **Chapel and Dining Hall** Wren completed the Chapel in 1687, but it was not consecrated until 1691. The Sunday morning Parade Service is open to the public and is well worth attending. Be warned – it is well

attended both by In-Pensioners and the general public. It has a fine choir.

4 Chelsea Physic Garden "A garden in Chelsea, hidden away behind high walls" is how one writer described the Society of Apothecaries who founded these gardens in 1673. For many years it was not open to the public, being primarily used for the research. It now has regular opening days and times. There is an admission charge.

5 Cheyne Walk Taking its name from the Lords of Manor – the Cheyne Family – almost every house is of great architectural interest. Here lived George Eliot, John Camden Nield, a miser, who left his fortune to Queen Victoria, and other notables of the eighteenth and nineteenth centuries. A number of blue plaques tell of other famous persons who have lived here.

6 Church of the Holy Redeemer This Roman Catholic church was built in 1895 to the designs of George Goldie. Its supplementary dedication was added after the canonisation in 1935 of Sir Thomas More. Alas, modern day vandalism has necessitated caging-in the entire west end of the church.

7 Carlyle's House Thomas Carlyle, historian, lived here for fifty years and here wrote his famous books. His clothes are in the wardrobe and his soundproof study is in the attic. He escaped here from the hustle and bustle of everyday life. The building is now owned by the National Trust and is open to the public between April and October only.

8 Albert Bridge One of London's most picturesque bridges was designed by R.C. Ordish and completed by the Albert Bridge Company in 1873. Originally a toll bridge, it was acquired on behalf of the public and officially opened by the Prince of Wales in 1879.

9 Chelsea Embankment Completed in 1871 under the direction of the engineer Sir Joseph Bazalgette and built for the Metropolitan Board of Works. It stretches from Chelsea Bridge to the Albert Bridge, a distance of three quarters of a mile. Across the river is Battersea Park, once below the tidal level of the river, when market gardeners used to grow asparagus here.

10 Ranelagh Gardens In 1742 these gardens were opened on the site of the house owned by Lord Ranelagh. On his death the house and grounds were bought by a syndicate led by Mr Lacey, of Drury Lane Theatre, and Sir Thomas Robinson, M.P. In the centre, a Rotunda was erected into which 'every body that loves eating, drinking, staring or crowding' was admitted for one shilling. The Rotunda was pulled down in 1805. The gardens closed and became part of the grounds of the Royal Hospital.

Bus Route 23: Paddington to Portobello Market

Route Praed Street – Eastbourne Terrace – Bishop's Bridge Road – Westbourne Grove – Kensington Park Road – Elgin Crescent – Ladbroke Grove – Canal Way – Ladbroke Road – Kensal Road – Golbourne Road.

Start Bus stop outside Paddington underground station (Circle and District lines) in Praed Street.

Finish Trellick Towers, Kensal Road. Request bus stop.

Time Allow ten to fifteen minutes.

Bus No. 23

Return 27 from Pembridge Villas (at the end of Portobello Road).

Tickets To cover Zones 1 and 2.

One of the most popular street markets of London is the one that stretches the whole length of **Portobello Road**. On Fridays and Saturdays it extends through to Golbourne Road and has a multi-racial flavour, both in produce and in population. The bus stops outside the underground station in Praed Street (Circle and District Lines), and opposite the Great Western Hotel with Paddington (British Rail) station behind it. The station is the terminus for the former Great Western Railway that was built by Isambard Kingdom Brunel between 1850 and 1854. The hotel was built by Philip Hardwick and was opened on 9th June 1854. Look up at the pediment, by John Thomas, illustrating Peace, Plenty, Industry and Science. Shortly after leaving the station the bus turns right along Eastbourne Terrace with its row of modern offices on the left and the side of the railway station on the right.

At the end of the terrace is Bishop's Bridge Road. Here the bus turns to the left and Hallfield Estate is on the left. It was described by Ian Nairn in *Modern Buildings in London* as being "a courageous attempt at a complete social unit, with schools and an evening institute as well as the flats, which are themselves varied in height and group". Its designers were Lindsey Drake, Denys Lasdun and Tecton all of whom went on to be members of the Tecton practice of architects. The estate shows the distinct influence of the Bauhaus Movement of Architecture that started in the 1930s in Germany. There are fifteen large blocks of flats and some smaller ones built in a well-landscaped environment. "The sheer size of the complex is somewhat overbearing." During its building in the 1950s it attracted visiting architects from all over the world.

In Queensway, on the left, can be seen William Whiteley's Store. This shop pioneered the development of departmental stores in London. It ceased trading as a store in 1981, but re-opened later as a shopping centre. There is a modern legend told that had Adolf Hitler conquered London in the Second World War, he intended to make the store his headquarters. History and fate made it otherwise. To visit the store, alight from the bus in Westbourne Grove, just past the end of Queensway. Westbourne Grove is a mixture of shops and restaurants and runs through to Kensington Park Road where the bus turns right. Just before the end of the Grove, the route passes through one part of Portobello Road. Do not get off the bus here! At least not on Fridays or Saturdays – the best is yet to come!

On the left can be seen the gardens of the houses that mark the site of the Hippodrome race track that flourished here in the 1800s. It closed in 1841 and the property developers moved in.

After turning into Elgin Crescent, the bus turns right into Ladbroke Grove. Here, during the August Bank Holiday week-end, the now world-famous Caribbean Carnival takes place. This great annual event started in 1959 as the race riots of the early 1950s reached their peak. It is a strong contrast to those riots and provides a celebration of traditional West Indian culture for all to enjoy.

A bridge carries the City and Hammersmith underground railway and the A40 (M) over Ladbroke Road. Here, under the elevated roadway on the right, part of the street market can be seen at weekends. On a corner shortly after the bridge is the parish church of St Michael & All Angels that was consecrated in 1871. The style of the building is described as being "Romanesque of the Rhine" and was designed by J. and J.S. Edmeston. A contrast to the church is the modern North Kensington Fire Station on another corner further along the road.

Just past the railway bridge is Canal Way. This leads to and from one of Sainsbury's many stores in London. Across the roadway is Kensal Road which runs alongside the canal – glimpses of which can be seen to the left. At the end of the road stands Trellick Tower, a modern high-rise block of flats. Alight from the bus here. Note that it is a request stop and requires the bell to be rung once – but only once!

Ahead lies **Golbourne Road** (Fridays and Saturdays only) Street Market. Here there is a mixture of fruit and vegetables; clothing, new and old; and a fair sprinkling of antiques to be found on the stalls. The shops, too, offer a variety of goods, edible and otherwise. The continuation of Golbourne Road is Portobello Road, and if you cannot find what you want in the antique line here – then it isn't in London! A casual stroll takes about forty to forty five minutes, but a more detailed look takes much longer. Allow yourself plenty of time, including a refreshment break along the way. Good hunting and shopping!

Bus Route 274: Marble Arch to London Zoo and Primrose Hill

Route Portman Street – Portman Square – Gloucester Place – Dorset Square – Gloucester Place – Park Road – Prince Albert Road – Primrose Hill.

Start Portman Street.

Finish London Zoo.

Time Allow ten to fifteen minutes for the journey.

Bus No. 274

Return Either by bus No. 274 from the stop opposite 33 Prince Albert Road or, during the summer months, by canal narrow boat to Little Venice.

Tickets Travelcard to cover Zones 1 and 2.

A visit to **London Zoo** in Regent's Park is a must for all visitors. The bus stop is in Portman Street, off Oxford Street, by the side of the Littlewoods store. Shortly after leaving the bus stop, Portman Square, with its private garden in the centre, is reached. Built between 1764 and 1784, the square when it was first laid out was described as being *"on the outskirts of the town"*. Today the square and its surrounding streets and squares are totally absorbed into the vast area called London. In the north-west corner stands the Portman Inter-Continental Hotel. On this site, in the late eighteenth century, Robert Adam, the fashionable architect of the day, built a town house for Mrs Elizabeth Montagu. The lady was a notable philanthropist who on May Day every year entertained the local chimney-sweeps and their apprentices to a celebratory dinner. The meal consisted of roast beef of England and plum (Christmas?) pudding, and was thoroughly enjoyed by all those taking part in the event. All that is left of the house can be seen at Kenwood House, Hampstead – a fine pair of gate-piers. Today the west side of the square is occupied by the Churchill Hotel. The remoteness of the area in the eighteenth century is reflected in the fact that in 1799 a Roman Catholic chapel was established in Portman Close behind Portman Square. Erected by French emigres and called the Chapel Royal of France, the consecration ceremony was attended by sixteen mitred bishops. It continued to serve the French community throughout the nineteenth century, by which time the Catholic hierarchy had been re-established, and Catholics were able to worship openly once more.

Leave the square by way of Gloucester Place where, in the main, the houses are now used as offices or hotels with a few let as flats. Number 48 was the home of John Robert Godley from 1852 to his death in 1861. Deeply distressed at the plight of the famine in Ireland, he put forward a plan for mass emigration to the colonies. Together with Edward Gibbon Wakefield, the colonial statesman and pamphleteer, Godley founded the City of Canterbury in New Zealand. Charles Dickens lived at 57 for a few months in 1863 after his return from Paris, and at number 65 (formerly 90), Wilkie Collins began writing "The Moonstone", the first detective story ever published. Numbers 74 and 99 both have connections with the Barretts of Wimpole Street. The former was the family home until they moved to Wimpole Street, and the latter was home to Elizabeth between 1835 and 1838.

On the corner of Gloucester Place and Marylebone Road is the Westminster Council House, the meeting place for the duly elected members of the Westminster City Council. Gloucester Place crosses Marylebone Road and shortly afterwards enters Dorset Square. As the bus passes the end of the central, private garden, look for the two brown plaques on the small summer house. They record the site of the first cricket ground founded here in 1787 by Thomas Lord, a Yorkshire man and the founder of the Marylebone Cricket Club (MCC), now the Mecca for cricket lovers. Lord's moved to its present site in 1811, after which the houses were built around the square. During the Second World War, 1939-1945, number one, on the right, was the headquarters of the Free French. A plaque at the side of the doorway records the men and women who set off from here on missions to occupied France during that war. The roadway continues northwards to Park Road where it turns to the left. The roadway runs along the outside of Regent's Park with the back of the architecturally famous Nash Terraces on the right. Shortly, on the right, is the Windsor Castle Public House, and next to it the Royal College of Obstetricians & Gynaecologists. The College houses an interesting collection of seventeenth century surgical instruments. It was founded in 1929 for "the encouragement of the study and the improvement of the practice of obstetrics and gynaecology, which should be inseparably interwoven". At Hanover Gate, on the right, is the London Central Mosque which was designed by Frederick Gibberd. It cost over one million pounds, with contributions coming from all over the Islamic world. It is open daily to "respectful visitors", except on Fridays – that is kept as a Sabbath (day of rest and worship).

Ahead lies the roundabout that leads to Prince Albert Road. Immediately on the left is the present day **Lord's Cricket Ground**. Immediately afterwards is the parish church of **St John's Wood**. Built in 1813-1814 as a chapel of ease to the parish church of St Marylebone, it achieved parochial status in 1952. It was designed by Thomas Hardwick. The site is not without a story or two from the past. It was once a plague pit and the crossroads here were used to bury murderers, suicides and highwaymen – in unconsecrated ground. In 1823 a murderer was buried here with a stake through his stomach! In the churchyard is the grave of Joanna Southcott, the "prophetess and fanatic". After her dreams were published, she gathered around her followers who would hang on to every last word that she spoke. In 1802 she announced that she would give birth to a spiritual man – Shiloh. She died in 1814 of a brain disease and was buried under the name of Goddard. Also buried here is John Sell Cotman, the landscape painter who was a leading member of the Norwich School of Painting. In 1834 he was appointed the Drawing Master at King's College in the Strand. Opposite the church, on the right, is a figure of St George slaying the dragon – it is a War Memorial. On the right is Regent's Park, some 194 hectares (480 acres) of public open space. The park has much to offer visitors, including the London Zoological Gardens.

Prince Albert Road leads out of the roundabout where high blocks of flats overlook the park. At number 33 there is a blue plaque commemorating Edward Goodrich Acheson, the inventor, scientist, and industrialist, who lived here between 1912 and 1915.

Just past the house is the bus stop at the foot of Primrose Hill. Alight here to visit the hill and the London Zoological Gardens.

Primrose Hill was "once covered with a medieval forest full of lairs, coverts and game". All that, and much more, was cleared away in the sixteenth century and the hill converted into a pleasant meadow. From the top of the hill, 63 metres (206ft) in height, on a clear day London can be seen spread out like a blanket. It is the meeting point at the Winter and Spring Solstice of the Members of the Ancient Order of Druids who perform their age-old ceremonies here. Since 1841, when it was "purchased by an exchange of money and land at Windsor with Eton College", it has been an open public space. There are at least three boundary marks on the hill, one metal and two stones. These mark the boundary of the former Parish of St Pancras (S P P 1821 is clearly shown on one of them). At the foot of the hill there is a space set aside for the playing of Petanque (or boule as it is more popularly called). It is a ball-and-target game similar to bowls and is played tossing a metal bowl towards the jack. There is also an Exercise or Trim Trail for the athletic type, as well as a children's play area.

Cross the road to London Zoo, and follow the signs. In 1826 the Zoological Society of London was founded by Sir Stamford Raffles, colonial governor and founder of the island of Singapore, and other

London Zoo

notable persons including Sir Humphrey Davy, inventor of the Davy Safety Lamp for miners. The following year, 1827, Decimus Burton laid out an area of Regent's Park for the Society. The zoo is not only one of the major tourist attractions of London, but also a major research centre. Early regulations stipulated that whips must be left behind at the ticket office, but ladies were allowed to carry their parasols, providing they did not poke the animals with them! Redevelopment plans are now in progress to take the zoo into the next millennium with the watchwords "Conservation in Action".

An alternative return journey is by water-bus from the canal side to Little Venice, Paddington, or to Camden Lock in the opposite direction. Both destinations are on, or are near to, bus routes to various parts of London. To return by the number 274 bus, walk back to Prince Albert Road and wait at the bus stop opposite number 33. This will return you to Oxford Street, close to Marble Arch.

The Royal Naval College, Greenwich

Bus Route 177: Greenwich to the Thames Barrier

Route Greenwich High Road – Greenwich High Street – College Approach – King William Walk – Romney Road – Trafalgar Road – Woolwich Road – Harden's Manor Way.

Start Greenwich (BR) Station.

Finish Thames Barrier.

Time Allow twenty minutes for the journey to Greenwich by train from Charing Cross main-line station and another twenty minutes for the bus journey.

Bus No 177.

Return Bus 177 and then British Rail to central London.
Alternative return journey to central London: walk under the river, by way of the Greenwich pedestrian tunnel, to the Isle of Dogs. Use the Docklands Light Railway's Island Gardens Station and then travel either to the Bank or Tower Gateway stations.

Tickets Travelcard to cover all Zones. Note All Zones Travelcard allows travel on buses, underground trains, Docklands Light Railway and the British Rail trains.

The bus stop for the number 177 is a short walk from the station. Turn right on leaving the forecourt. On the opposite side of the road stands Queen Elizabeth College, founded by William Lambard in 1576 as almshouses for citizens of Greenwich. A severe outbreak of the bubonic plague threatened the college in the seventeenth century and caused the place to be closed. It survived, however, and was rebuilt in its present form in 1819. It can house forty persons, and its tiny chapel is still in use throughout the year. Shortly after leaving the station bus stop, the route passes the parish church dedicated to the twenty-eighth Archbishop of Canterbury, St Alphege. He died as the result of being hit on the head by an axe, having been caught up in a drunken brawl of marauding Danes. The church was designed by Nicholas Hawksmoor and was another of the churches built under the Fifty New Churches Act of 1711.

On entering Greenwich High Street the bus enters the one-way system of roads and turns right into College Approach and right again into King William Walk. At the end of the Walk is Romney Road. On the right is the **National Maritime Museum** and **The Queens' House,** and on the left the former Royal Naval College.

From Romney Road the bus travels along Trafalgar Road, past the Greenwich District Hospital, on the right, and under the fly-over roadway that leads to the Blackwall Tunnel under the river. When The Victoria public house, on the left, is reached, push the bell to stop the bus at the next request stop. This is just past Unity Way that leads down to the river and the **Thames Barrier.** Described as being the eighth wonder of the modern world, the barrier was built as part of the flood defence scheme for protecting London against the rising water levels and tidal surges. Work was begun on the barrier in 1972 and not completed until 1982. It consists of ten movable steel gates. When raised, the four main gates stand as high as a five storey house and as wide as the opening of Tower Bridge, and weigh over 3,700 tonnes. There is a very interesting Visitors' Centre.

A stroll by the riverside will open up vistas both across and along the river. Moored close by the river pier that brings boats to and from Greenwich is the Russian submarine Foxtrot U-475 which is also open to visitors for an admission fee. "Take this unique opportunity to delve into the secretive and sinister world of a Russian Submarine – the only one in the UK". The U-475 was in active service with the Russian Baltic Fleet until 1st April 1994 and had twenty seven years of naval service. As an alternative return journey, why not take the short boat trip back to Greenwich from the pier?

Bus Route D9: King William Street to the Asda store, Isle of Dogs

Route King William Street – East Cheap – Great Tower Street – Tower Hill – East Smithfield – Highway – Butcher Row – Commercial Road – West India Dock Road – West Ferry Circus – Cartier Circus – Cabot Place – Canada Square – Cabot Place – Cabot Circus – West Ferry Circus – South Dock and City Canal Basin – Marsh Wall – South Quay – Manchester Road – Island Gardens Station(Docklands Light Railway) – Mud Chute – Asda store.

Start King William Street (nearest underground station – Bank).

Finish Asda store, Isle of Dogs, or Island Gardens Station (Docklands Light Railway).

Time Allow forty five minutes

Bus No. D9 usually operates in the evenings or when the Docklands Light Railway is not working

Return Either by the D9 bus or the Docklands Light Railway from Island Gardens Station.

Tickets Travel card to cover Zones one and two.

King William Street commemorates William IV who opened the London Bridge of 1831 when the roadway formed part of the approaches to the new bridge. Most of the buildings that line the roadway today date from this century. As the bus crosses the road junction at the end of the street, look to the right where the new **London Bridge** opened by Her Majesty the Queen Elizabeth II in 1972 can be seen.

The bus now enters East Cheap where, on the left, is the Guild Church of St Margaret Pattens on the corner of Rood Lane. In medieval times a tall cross with the figure of Christ stood here and the faithful would bring their offerings towards the building and maintenance of the church. At the time of the English Reformation the cross was destroyed as being a "popish idol of worship". Destroyed in the Great Fire of 1666, the church was rebuilt to the designs of Sir Christopher Wren in the late seventeenth century. Just past the church, East Cheap becomes Great Tower Street. On the right-hand side is the parish church of **All-Hallows-by-the-Tower**. There has been a church on this site since the seventh century, a fact that was proved at the time of the church's restoration after being bombed in the last war. A late seventh century arch was discovered built into the present seventeenth century west tower. In medieval times a shrine in honour of St Mary of Barking (early patrons of the church were the Abbesses of Barking Abbey) was erected. The shrine attracted many pilgrims and a Brotherhood was formed to pray at, and to maintain the shrine. Both statue and fraternity ceased at the time of the English Reformation of the sixteenth century. Today the church ministers to the needs of the city workers and an eclectic congregation. While serving as a padre in the First World War, 1914-1918, the Reverend "Tubby" Clayton established at Poperinghe near Ypres a Christian oriented Centre. They met in Talbot House, or in signallers' jargon, Toc H. Today this Fellowship is world-wide, but still regards this church as being the focal point of the organisation. In the church there is a tomb-like memorial to "Tubby", and in the crypt chapel his ashes rest behind the cross of the altar.

On the right-hand side is the Tower of London, while from the bus stop on the left can be seen large pieces of the City wall. From here the bus crosses over the next road junction and moves down East Smithfield to the Highway. On the right is an entrance to St Katharine's Dock. On the left is the parish church of **St George in the East** that was built under the Fifty New Churches for London Act of 1711. It was designed by Nicholas Hawksmoor and rebuilt after severe damage during the last war. The outer walls were retained, but a courtyard was arranged within them, creating a smaller church at the east end of the building. Around the courtyard at first floor level, two flats have been built for the clergy and below there are rooms for meetings. Beneath the church, in the crypt (cellar), a large hall has been created, complete with a stage capable of being used for rehearsals by many West End Shows. The coffins and other contents were carefully removed and reburied in another place away from the church.

Ahead lies the Limehouse Link, a new road tunnel built as part of the approaches to the Docklands' developments. The bus turns to the left along Butcher Row where on the right-hand side can be seen the buildings of the Royal Foundation of Saint Katharine. Founded originally on the site of **St Katharine's Dock**, the Foundation was scheduled to be dissolved at the time of the Dissolution of the Monasteries in 1539. However, due to its status, and most certainly to the influence of Henry VIII's sixth, and final wife, it survived. It stayed on its first site until progress intervened and the land was acquired to build the docks that still bears its name. The Foundation moved to Regent's Park, where it remained until 1948 when it moved to its present site.

At the junction to Commercial Road the bus turns left and continues on its journey towards Docklands. Along the way to West Ferry Road, look out on the right-hand side and see the **Limehouse Basin**, the river end of the Grand Union Canal that starts its journey southward from Birmingham. The basin has been partly filled in recent years and housing built on the new land. It is also used as a marina for privately owned boats. Shortly after the basin is the Limehouse Public Library with the statue of Clement Attlee by Frank Forster. He was elected Leader of the Labour Party in 1935 and went on to serve as Deputy Prime Minister under Sir Winston Churchill during the Second World War. Later he became Prime Minister in the Labour Government of 1945. He introduced National Health and National Insurance and gave India its independence during his term of office. He died in 1967. The statue was unveiled by the late Lord Wilson of Rievaulx in November 1988.

The parish church of Limehouse, dedicated to St Anne, was built between 1712 and 1720 to the designs of Nicholas Hawksmoor. It was also built from the funds of the Fifty Churches Act. West India Dock Road leads into the Docklands Development area that has been described as being " an exciting example of late twentieth century architecture set among landscaped squares, gardens and water promenades". And such it certainly is – for Londoners and visitors alike. Dominating London's skyline is **Canary Wharf's** tower block. This is the tallest building in London. Originally designed to rise 305 metres (1000ft) into the sky, it was realised that it would interfere with 'planes landing at the City Airport and it was reduced to 245 metres (800ft). The London Docklands Development Corpo-

Canary Wharf tower from Millwall Dock

ration leaflet boldly declares, "Don't go home without seeing it." That is excellent advice and should be acted upon!

The bus route takes the passenger on a short conducted tour by way of West Ferry Circus, Cartier Circus, Cabot Place and Canada Square before returning to West Ferry Circus. Then the route moves off to South Dock and the City Canal and Marsh Wall. There is a visitors' centre close to Crossharbour station. Here you can wander around the exhibition "Today, yesterday and to-morrow" and watch a thirteen minute video presentation, as well as collect leaflets and information regarding the development. On certain days a two hour coach tour of the area leaves from the Centre. Meanwhile, the D9 travels on to Manchester Road and the pre-development area built by Thomas Cubitt in the nineteenth century. Note The Cubitt Arms public house en route. The parish church of Christ Church, Cubitt Town is on the left. Built in 1852 by William Cubitt to the designs of Frederick Johnston, architect, to "serve as the spiritual centre of Cubitt Town". Although predominantly made of brick, the stone that was used came from medieval London Bridge. Like most London churches it suffers from vandalism and has closed doors except for those occasions when there is a church watcher on duty. It is, however, often open during the late morning Monday to Friday, with the vicarage next door for the anxious to enquire for the key.

Island Gardens Station, on the left, is the terminus for the Docklands Light Railway and also the place to alight for those wishing to visit Greenwich by way of the pedestrian tunnel under the river at this point. For those wishing to continue by bus the D9 travels along Manchester Road to East Ferry Road where it turns right and the journey terminates in the car park of the Asda store. A short walk from the terminus is Mudchute Farm where sheep peacefully graze and horse-riding is available. A descriptive notice board in the farm area tells the origin of the Mudchute.

Appendix A: Southwark Cathedral

This cathedral is London's second most important example of medieval architecture after Westminster Cathedral. Here, John Harvard was baptised and the university that he founded maintains the Harvard Chapel in his memory. It is also the burial place of several actors who performed at the Globe Theatre. Its principal features are listed here (see plan):

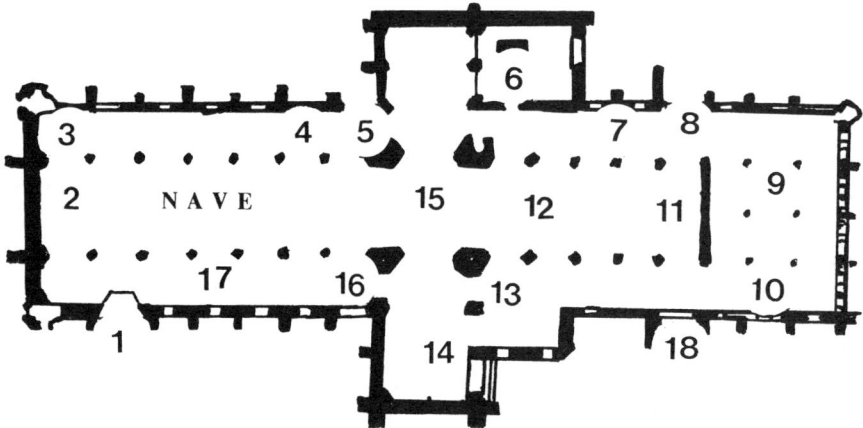

1   **South-west doorway** Before entering the cathedral look to the left where can be seen a piece of wall from the Roman villa that was on this site. Note the "Herring-bone" arrangement of the tiles.
2   **Font** The Canon Law of the Church of England states: "the font shall stand near the principal entrance as conveniently may be.." It is here the Sacrament of Baptism is carried out.
3   **Roof bosses** These roof bosses were high in the roof of the church, and have often been described as being the "Poor Man's Bible". They often tell the biblical story in stone or wood.
4   **John Gower's tomb** John Gower was Poet Laureate to Richard II and Henry IV, and is recognised as being the "first English Poet".
5   **Doorway to vestry** This leads to the private vestries but just behind the right-hand door can be seen an original across from the 12th century church

Appendix A: Southwark Cathedral

6 Harvard chapel Dedicated to St John the Divine it is also known as the Harvard Chapel in memory of John Harvard. Founder of Harvard University in America who was born in Southwark, and baptised in this church.

7 Trehearne monument The inscription reads "An epitaph upon John Trehearne, gentleman portar (sic) to King James I". A note in the records reads "John Trehearne of Bankside pays double for withholding his tythes". A lax payer of taxes!

8 Effigy of knight Lying in a recess is the 13th century wooden effigy of a crusading knight

9 Retro-choir Here is a good place to sit, rest, and ponder over all he thousands of people who have passed through these walls in the last seven hundred years.

10 Consistory Court A court under the jurisdiction of a bishop where misdemeanours of clergy and parishes can be heard – and judged. Here Prebendary John Rogers was tried, for heresy, and found guilty.

11 High altar screen The great screen behind the high altar was first erected during the rule of Richard Fox, Bishop of Winchester, in the sixteenth century. The figures are modern.

12 Choir In between the choir stalls lie buried Edmund Shakespeare and other members of the Theatre of the seventeenth century.

13 Roman pavement Another reminder of the Roman villa that once stood on this site. Nearby can be seen a piece of statuary that was found in a well in the crypt of the church.

14 Beaufort's arms To the side of the doorway here are the arms of Cardinal Henry Beaufort, son of John of Gaunt, who was Bishop of Winchester in the fifteenth century

15 Nave altar In keeping with the modern tradition an altar, bishop's chair, etc, has been placed under the crossing. In the roof are some of the original roof bosses.

16 Shakespeare monument The reclining figure of William Shakespeare lies in front of a panorama of Bankside in the sixteenth and seventeenth century. Above is a modern stained glass window depicting characters from his plays.

17 Bookstall No visitor to any cathedral is complete without a call at the bookstall. Here can be purchased books, souvenirs, etc.

18 George Gwilt's tomb Gwilt's restoration of the medieval portions of the cathedral in the 19th century eventually led to the rebuilding of the "new nave".

Key to the reredos (stone screen behind altar)

```
┌─────────────────────────────────────────────────────────┐
│  1 │ 2 │ 3 │ 4 │ 5      │ 6   │ 7 │ 8 │ 9 │ 10         │
│    │   │   │   │    A   │     │   │   │   │            │
├─────────────────────────────────────────────────────────┤
│ 11 │12 │13 │14 │ 15     │ 16  │17 │18 │19 │ 20         │
│    │   │   │   │    B   │     │   │   │   │            │
├─────────────────────────────────────────────────────────┤
│    │21 │22 │ Angels  │ Angels │ 23 │ 24 │               │
│    │   │   │ Apostles│Apostles│    │    │               │
│    │   │   │   C  │ D │  E    │    │    │               │
│ 25 │   │   │   F  │   │  G    │    │    │  26           │
│    │   │   │      │ H │       │    │    │               │
└─────────────────────────────────────────────────────────┘
```

1   **Bishop Anthony** Thorold Bishop of Winchester, 1890-1895 raised the money for the rebuilding of the "new" nave.

2   **Saint Olave** King of Norway in 1016 after his conversion to Christianity

3   **William of Wykeham** Bishop of Winchester, 1367-1404 was also the Lord High Chancellor He holds a model of Winchester Cathedral and Palace in his hands

4   **Cardinal Henry Beaufort** Second son of John of Gaunt and uncle of Henry V. Bishop of Winchester 1405-1447, described as being "a militant ecclesiastic scheming and unscrupulous"

5   **St Paul** The Apostle of the Gentiles. Born at Tarsus, and beheaded in Rome c 67 AD.

Appendix A: Southwark Cathedral

6   **St Augustine of Hippo** Patron saint of the Order of Augustinian Canons, whose writings include "Confessions of St Augustine".

7   **William Gifford** Bishop of Winchester 1100 – 1129 Founded St Mary Overie and built a bishop's palace here. He was the builder of the Norman church.

8   **Aldgood** First prior of St Mary Overie. He died in 1130.

9   Saint Justus First Bishop of Rochester he came to England with St Augustine of Canterbury.

10 **Edward Talbot** First Bishop of Southwark, he was enthroned on 20th June 1905.

11 **Prebendary John Rogers** Rector of the parish church of Saint Sepulchre-without-Newgate he was the first Protestant martyr in the reign of Queen Mary.. He was burnt alive at Smithfield, after having been found guilty of heresy. His trial took place in the retro-choir where a stained glass window tells his story.

12 **Saint Swithun** Bishop of Winchester, 852-863, he established a College of Priests here that replaced the original nuns in 852. His shrine in Winchester was one of the most popular in England.

13 **Saint Thomas of Canterbury** Archbishop of Canterbury, 1162-1170 Pilgrims on their way to his shrine in Canterbury Cathedral are said to have visited the church on their pilgrimage. The rest of the screen is made up of figures which show Christ (A & B).

14 St Margaret of Antioch Southwark's former parish church was dedicated to this saint. It was closed when priory was dissolved and became the parish church.

15 **Saint Peter** Leader of the Apostles who died, upside down on a cross in Rome, c.64 AD.

16 **Saint John the Evangelist** The Harvard Chapel is dedicated to him. The youngest of the twelve Apostles. He lived to a great age and died at Ephesus, according to tradition.

17 **St Mary Magdalene** "Mary of Magdala" who was cured from being possessed by seven devils and became an ardent follower of Christ. He appeared to her in the Garden of the Gethsemane after His Resurrection.

18 **John Gower** The 'first English Poet', he lived and died in Southwark. Note the inkhorn and pen he carries.

19 **Peter des Roches** Bishop of Winchester, 1204-1238 He died at his "country retreat" at Farnham, then a palace for the bishops.

20 **Randall Davidson** Bishop of Winchester, 1893-1903 then Archbishop

of Canterbury from 1903-1928. Preached at the "opening of the 'new' nave in 1895.

21 **Rochester's diocesan arms** The cross is an allusion to St Andrew in whose honour the cathedral was originally dedicated. The shell is the sign of pilgrims.

22 **Canterbury coat of arms** They show the archbishop's crozier (cross) and the pallium that was placed over each archbishop's head when they were made archbishops.

23 **Winchester's coat of arms** The Keys of St Peter, crossed with the sword of St. Paul, to whom the cathedral is dedicated.

24 **Southwark's coat of arms** Based on the coat of arms of the Priory of St Mary Overie in Southwark. The mitre is a modern addition to the arms.

25 **Henry I** Fourth son of William the Conqueror he was once described as being a man of good business qualities who ruled with a firm hand.

26 **Edward VII** Eldest son of Victoria and Albert and who laid the foundation stone of the "new" nave in 1890.

A **Christ reigning in glory** depicting St Saviour which is part of the dedication of the cathedral.

B **Christ in humility**, sitting in His crib with Mary His Mother

C **Saint Jerome,** "among the greatest biblical scholars"

D **The Risen Christ**

E **St Gregory Nazianzen** was one of the four great Greek doctors of the Church. His discourses on the Holy Trinity earned him the title "the Theologian".

F **St Ambrose**, a lawyer by training, Bishop of Milan, and well-known in his time for the power of his sermons.

G **St Basil the Great** has been described as being the Father of Eastern Communal Life.

H **The High Altar**, where the main services of the church would have taken place. Today these have been moved to the nave altar under the crossing of the church. The altarpiece with the Latin and Greek Fathers, etc., were designed by the late Sir Ninian Comper in 1929, and the twelve Apostles by John Oldrid Scott.

Appendix A: Southwark Cathedral 141

Shakespeare Memorial Window

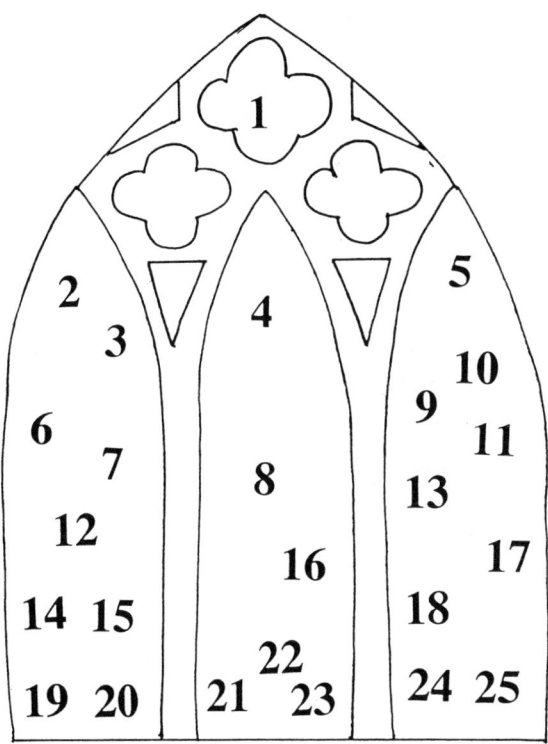

1. Shakespeare family coat of arms
2. Bottom and Puck "Midsummer Night's Dream"
3. Titania "Midsummer Night's Dream"
4. Ariel "The Tempest"
5. Romeo and Juliet "Romeo and Juliet"
6. Malvolio "Twelfth Night"
7. Olivia and Maria "Twelfth Night"
8. Prospero "The Tempest"
9. "My kingdom for a horse" "Richard III"
10. Richard II "Richard II"

11 Othello "Othello"
12 Falstaff "Henry IV, parts one and two"
13 King Lear "King Lear"
14 Portia "The Merchant of Venice"
15 Jacques and Touchstone "As You Like It"
16 Caliban "The Tempest"
17 Lady Macbeth "Macbeth"
18 Hamlet "Hamlet" Seven Ages of Man
19 The infant – "mewling and puking" in the nurse's arms
20 The "whinning" schoolboy.. creeping like a snail unwillingly to school
21 The Lover, sighing like a furnace
22 A Soldier, full of strange oaths
23 The Justice, in fair round belly with good capon lined
24 The lean and slipper's pantaloon
25 Second childishness, and mere oblivion, sans teeth, sans eyes, sans taste, sans everything.

Appendix B: Attractions and Sightseeing Tours

In addition to the services of London Transport, there are a number of other companies who offer sightseeing tours of the Capital. Details of their activities can be obtained from the Tourist Information Centre at Victoria Station and the British Rail Travel Centre in Regent Street. They operate a "hop-on, hop-off" service whereby for a ticket that covers twenty-four hours, it is possible to get on and off the vehicle in order to visit places of interest. The following are places you may wish to visit.

1. **Marble Arch** was erected in 1827 to form a ceremonial entrance to Buckingham Palace. It was designed by the architect John Nash and is a copy of the triumphal arch in Rome that commemorates the Roman Emperor Constantine. Only senior members of the Royal family are allowed to pass through its portals, together with the King's Troop, Royal Artillery.

2. **Apsley House** stands at the opposite end of Park Lane from Marble Arch and was the home of the First Duke of Wellington. It was built between 1771 and 1778, to the designs of Robert Adam for Henry Bathurst. The Duke bought it from his brother, Lord Wellesley, for £42,000 in 1817, at which time he faced the brick house with Bath stone. The house was given to the Nation in 1947, and it opened as the Wellington Museum in 1952. It has recently been reopened after an extensive refurbishment programme. It is well worth a visit.

3. **Buckingham Palace** is the London home of Her Majesty the Queen. Here, daily in the summer and alternate days in the winter, the Changing of the Guard can be seen. The building was practically rebuilt in the time of George IV by John Nash and has been added to since that time. In all there are some six hundred rooms in the palace, some of which are open to the general public during the months of August and September each year. There is an admission fee.

4. **Victoria Station** is the main terminus for the Southern Region of British Rail. As part of the extensions of the railway system of the United Kingdom, the London, Brighton and South Coast Railway Company extended their line across the Thames in the 1850s. The Grosvenor Bridge, the first railway bridge over the river, was built to

144 London Bus-Top Tourist

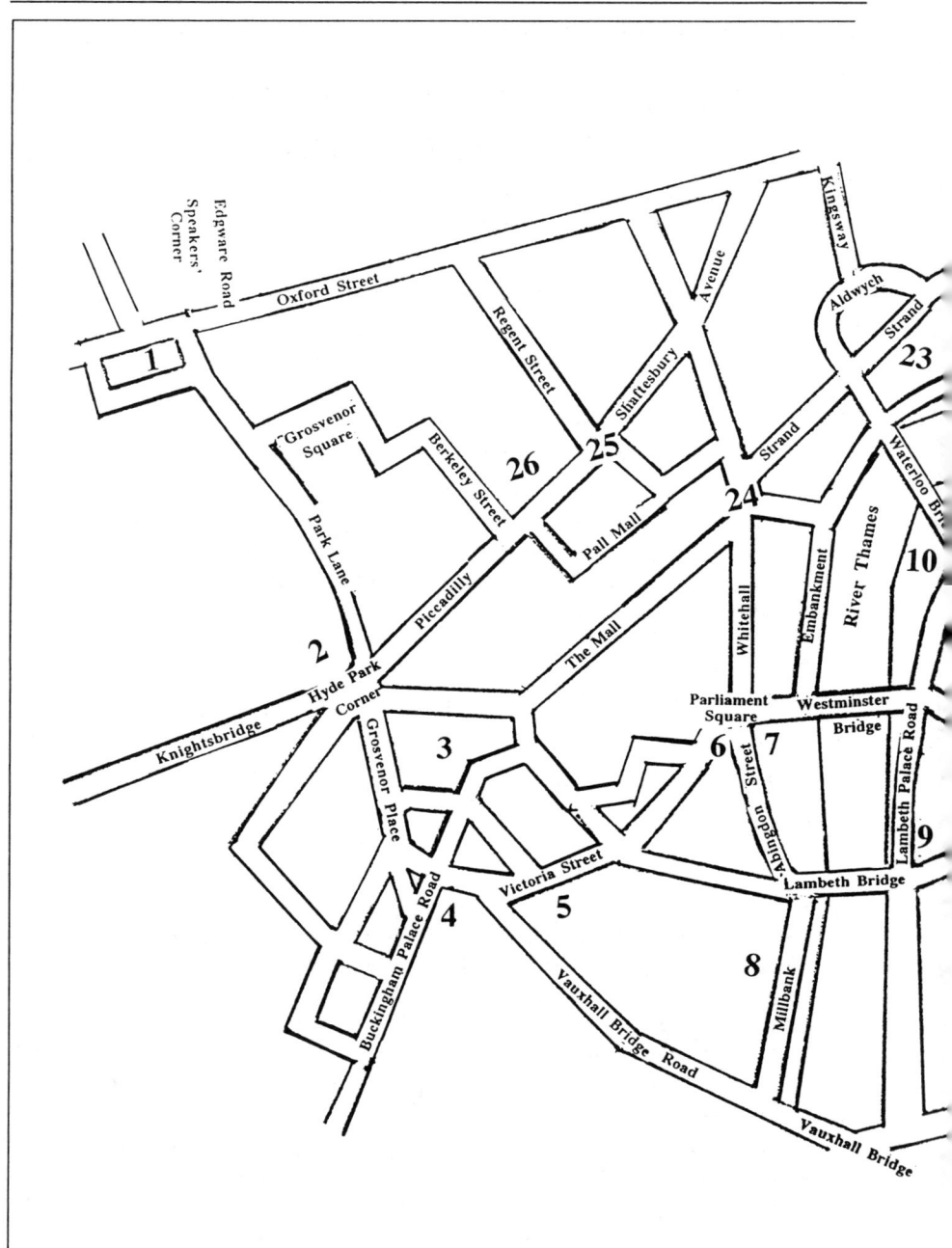

Appendix B: Attractions and Sightseeing Tours

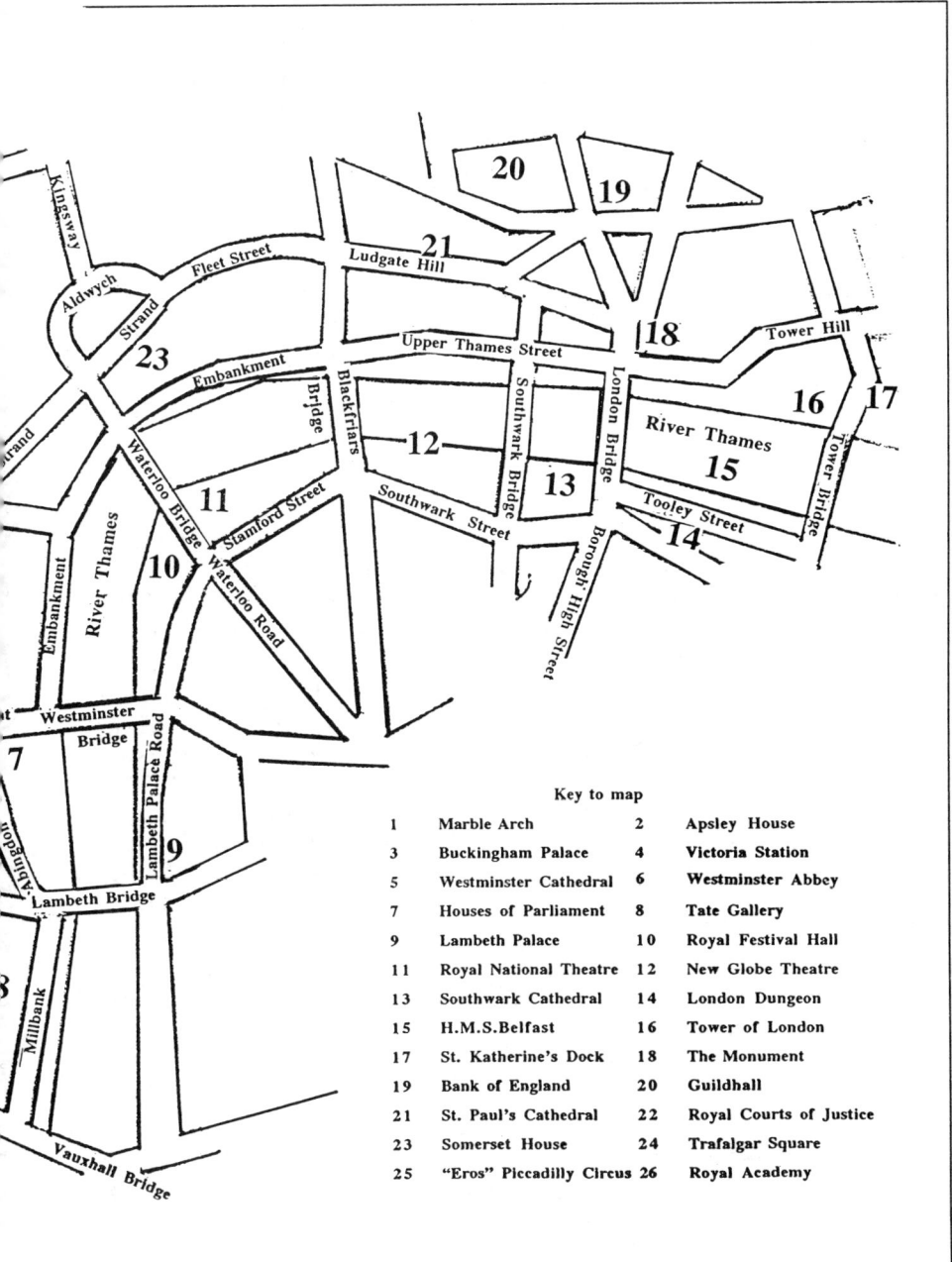

Key to map

1	Marble Arch	2	Apsley House
3	Buckingham Palace	4	Victoria Station
5	Westminster Cathedral	6	Westminster Abbey
7	Houses of Parliament	8	Tate Gallery
9	Lambeth Palace	10	Royal Festival Hall
11	Royal National Theatre	12	New Globe Theatre
13	Southwark Cathedral	14	London Dungeon
15	H.M.S. Belfast	16	Tower of London
17	St. Katherine's Dock	18	The Monument
19	Bank of England	20	Guildhall
21	St. Paul's Cathedral	22	Royal Courts of Justice
23	Somerset House	24	Trafalgar Square
25	"Eros" Piccadilly Circus	26	Royal Academy

bring the trains nearer to the West End. At the same time, the Grosvenor Hotel was erected alongside the station buildings. The London, Chatham and Dover Railway Company were also looking for a new terminus and built theirs on the eastern side of the Brighton line. Both companies remained separate entities until the formation of the Southern Railway Company in 1923. In 1948 all railway companies were nationalised and the company became the Southern Region of British Railways.

5 **Westminster Cathedral** was the first Roman Catholic cathedral to be built in England for over three hundred years, since the Reformation. It was designed by John Francis Bentley in the style of Early Christian Byzantine in order not to confuse it with Westminster Abbey at the other end of Victoria Street. Dedicated to the Precious Blood of Our Lord Jesus Christ, its structure is made entirely of handmade bricks and without any reinforced steel frame to support it.

6 **Westminster Abbey** – there has been an abbey here for over nine hundred years. Tradition claims that it was founded by King Sigbert of the East Saxons in the seventh century and that St Peter returned to earth for one night to consecrate it. Today the building is looking in an almost pristine state having been meticulously restored over the past three decades. It is certainly one of the greatest mediaeval churches in the kingdom, if not in Europe.

7 **Houses of Parliament** – the Royal Palace of St Stephen at Westminster was first built by Edward the Confessor in the eleventh century. After his death in 1066 it was lived in by William the Conqueror, whose son, Rufus, added the Great Hall that still survives today. In 1834 a disastrous fire severely damaged or destroyed most of the buildings. Sir Charles Barry, the architect, won the competition to design and build its replacement. Thus, a new building for the "Mother of Parliaments" came into being and, in spite of wars and strifes, remains loyal to its foundations.

8 **Tate Gallery,** Millbank was opened in 1897 on the site of the former Millbank Prison and was designed by Sidney J.R. Smith in "an eclectic neo-classical style". It houses the important national collection of British paintings from the sixteenth century. The Turner Collection is now housed in the Clore Gallery that has been added to the original building.

9 **Lambeth Palace** has been the London home of the Archbishop of Canterbury since the late twelfth century when Archbishop Baldwin purchased part of the Manor of Lambeth from its owners, the Convent of St Andrew at Rochester. His intention was to found a College of Priests here – but he never did! However, his successor, Archbishop

Hubert Walter, had a house built here for the monastic Order of Premonstratensian Canons, to which he attached one for himself. In its eight hundred years' history it has seen many famous people enter through its doors. The Tudor, sixteenth century, gatehouse was built during the time of Archbishop Morton, doubtless with some of the money that he raised in taxes. On his Visitations he would assess his host for tax purposes. If he was given a warm welcome and a handsome present, the host would be taxed heavily! If, on the other hand, his host was meagre in his entertaining, the archbishop would still tax him heavily on the premise that he was saving his money! It was known as "Morton's Fork" – if he didn't get your money one way, he got it the other!

10 **Royal Festival Hall** – built as part of the South Bank's Festival of Britain in 1951, it has remained as part of the South Bank Cultural Centre. It was designed by Sir Robert Matthew and J.L. Martin for the festival, and further developed by Sir Hubert Bennett ten years later. It seats 3,111 for recitals and 2,299 for ballet, when a theatrical proscenium arch is erected. An organ, designed by Ralph Downes, was installed in 1954.

11 **Royal National Theatre**, South Bank – after many starts and false starts, a National Theatre was opened here in 1976. The project was first suggested in 1948, and a foundation stone laid near the Royal Festival Hall during the festivities of 1951. It was designed by Sir Denys Lasdun and has three theatres under one roof. The Cottesloe is a small theatre that is highly adaptable and used for experimental plays, the Lyttelton is a proscenium styled theatre, and the Olivier has an open stage.

12 **New Globe Theatre,** Bankside, Southwark, was the dream of the late Sam Wanamaker to reconstruct Shakespeare's Globe Theatre near to where the Bard himself wrote and performed his plays. The theatre forms a part of the International Shakespeare Globe Centre that has been described as being " an entertainment, educational and cultural complex". Its thatched roof is the first of its kind since the 17th century and has been made according to the traditional process of that time.

13 **Southwark Cathedral**, by London Bridge – the original building was a Convent for nuns, who were later replaced by Augustinian Canons. After the Dissolution of the Monasteries Act of 1539, the building became a parish church, and finally in 1905 it was consecrated as the Cathedral Church of the Southwark (Anglican) diocese. The eastern part of the church is medieval and the western (nave) is nineteenth century. Shakespeare's brother, Edmund, lies buried in the choir, and a memorial to the Bard himself, together with a fine modern stained

glass window, recalls their connection with Southwark and Bankside. See Appendix A for plans of the cathedral, the great stone reredos behind the high altar and the window.

14   **London Dungeon,** Tooley Street. The leaflet reads, "Step back in time and journey through the darker side of European history....Can you survive the horrors of the London Dungeons?......This must be the world's most infamous museum of horror." It is not for the squeamish... but well worth a visit! A short distance from the Dungeon is the **Britain at War Experience** – an "adventure through the fury and danger of war-torn London".

15   **HMS *Belfast*** is the last surviving warship of World War II and was opened to the public in 1971, "giving a compelling insight into the nature of war at sea". There are fine views of the river, the Tower of London and Tower Bridge from the deck and bridge of the ship. It is now managed by the Imperial War Museum in Lambeth. The ticket that is given in exchange for the admission fee is also a guide to help visitors find their way around the seven decks of the ship.

16   **The Tower of London** was built at the instigation of William the Conqueror in order to protect the City of London from invaders. The central feature is the White Tower – the original Norman fortification that has been added to over the ensuing years. Here is housed the Royal (Coronation) Regalia. Over the years the Tower has been used to accommodate state prisoners, a royal menagerie and the Royal Mint, as well as acting as one of the many royal palaces for the monarchs of this country. Every night, just before 10pm, the Tower is locked for the night. Tickets for the Ceremony of the Keys can be obtained by writing to the Ceremony of the Keys Clerk, Queens House, Tower of London, London EC3N 4AB.But be warned, it is popular and there are only a limited number of tickets available. Write early!

17   **St Katharine's Dock**– here the Royal Foundation of St Katharine, now at No.2 Butcher Row, E14, was first founded in the twelfth century as a hospital for the poor of London. In 1828, after many protests from the local residents, St Katharine's Dock was opened as part of the expansion programme to increase the tonnage of shipping using the Port of London. After running at a loss for a number of years, the dock was closed in 1968 and sold by the Port of London Authority to the Greater London Council. Taylor Woodrow, a property development company bought the dock on a 125 year lease. In 1973 they erected the Tower Hotel on the riverside. The rest of the site contains offices, shops and housing, and the dock itself has become a marina. The Dickens Inn provides good food and drink with views across the waters.

18   Built in 1671 as a memorial to the Great Fire of London of 1666, the

Appendix B: Attractions and Sightseeing Tours

St Katharine's Dock

Monument was designed by Sir Christopher Wren. It stands 62 metres (202ft) high, and there are three hundred and eleven steps to be climbed to reach the balcony at the top of the column. The stone panels around the base relate the story of the fire in English and Latin. The panel on the west side is a bas-relief by Caius Gabriel Cibber, representing Charles II, with his brother the Duke of York, bringing relief to the City. There is an admission fee to climb to the top, from where splendid views across London may be seen. Since 1842 the balcony has been caged in after a servant girl threw herself over the railing.

19 In 1694 the **Bank of England** was founded by Royal Charter to raise the money needed by the Government in its war with France. The lower part of the building was erected in the eighteenth century to the designs of Sir John Soane. In the 1930s the rest of the bank was rebuilt by Sir Herbert Baker, with the entrance floor the work of Boris Anrep, who also decorated the Chapel of the Blessed Sacrament in Westminster Cathedral. While the Bank itself is not open to visitors, the excellent museum in Bartholomew Lane attracts many visitors. Admission is free and there are guide books to help the visitor understand the history of the Bank.

20 Much of the **Guildhall** dates from the fifteenth century. It is the centre of civic government of the City of London. Here the annual elections for the officers of the City take place, with those for the Lord Mayor for the ensuing year being the most important. There has been a hall here since "time out of memory" as John Stow, the sixteenth century historian, would say. It is the second largest hall of its kind in England, Westminster Hall being the largest. Apart from the top section, it has survived the Great Fire and the Blitz as few other buildings have done. It is open throughout the year for visitors, unless it is required for a function. There is no charge.

21 **St Paul's Cathedral** is the master-piece of Sir Christopher Wren who rebuilt it after the medieval one was severely damaged in the Great Fire of London in 1666. The cathedral is the chief church of the Diocese of London so the Bishop's throne can be seen here(cathedra meaning seat). There is an admission fee except at the times of services that occur at least three times a day. The view from the topmost gallery above the dome affords superb views across the whole of London, and on a fine day, beyond.

22 Standing at the city end of the Strand are the **Royal Courts of Justice** - the Law Courts that were opened in 1882 after having been housed in the Palace of Westminster for hundreds of years. Look out for the figure of Christ with his hand raised in blessing on the top of the gable of the Great Hall. The courts here deal with the non-criminal cases

(criminal cases are dealt with in the Central Criminal Courts, the "Old Bailey", in the City, close to Newgate.

23 **Somerset House**, in the Strand, takes its name from Edward Seymour, Duke of Somerset, "Protector Somerset", in the sixteenth century. He was the first guardian of the "boy king", Edward VI. After the duke's execution in 155, "he having exceeded his duties", the house became a royal palace when the Princess Elizabeth (later Elizabeth I) lived there. In the following century Charles I gave the house to his Queen, Henrietta Maria, who brought with her, from France, her own priests to say Mass. In the late eighteenth century the palace was demolished and shortly afterwards the present structure was erected to the designs of Sir William Chambers. Until 1973 the buildings were used for a variety of governmental and learned societies. Today the State Rooms are occupied by the Courtauld Art Gallery, and for an admission fee may be visited.

24 **Trafalgar Square** commemorates the great sea-battle won by Horatio, Lord Nelson on 21st October 1805, and is dominated by a 44 metres (145ft) high column on which a statue of Nelson stands.

25 Standing at the heart of the Empire is **Eros** – the memorial drinking fountain erected to the memory of the 7th Earl of Shaftesbury. The figure on the top is not the God of Erotica, but the Christian Angel of Charity, and is, in fact, a rebus on the Earl's title. The figure with an archer's bow has released an arrow (shaft) that has buried itself in some distant plot of ground – Shaftes+bury.

26 Founded in 1768, the **Royal Academy of Arts** is the oldest society in England devoted entirely to the fine arts. Foundation members included Joshua Reynolds (first President), Sir William Chambers (first Treasurer) as well as Paul Sandby, Thomas Gainsborough, Benjamin West (later to become the first American President of the Society), and Richard Wilson. It is housed in Burlington House, former home of the Earls of Burlington, and holds regular exhibitions of paintings and the arts, the most famous being the annual Summer Exhibition. There is an admission fee.

Appendix C: General Information

Telephone numbers

London Transport: 55, Broadway, Westminster, London, SW1. 0171-222-1234 (24 hours service)

Lost Property: London Transport, 200 Baker Street, London, NW1 5RZ. 0171-486-2496

Taxis: 0171-833-0996

Places of interest and opening times: *(F)*= free admission, *(C)*=entrance charge

Bank of England Museum: 0171-601-4878. Mon – Fri, 10am to 5pm; Sun, 11am to 5pm. *(F)*

Banqueting House, Whitehall: Mon – Sat, 9am to 5pm. *(C)*

British Museum, Great Russell Street: 0171-636-1555. Mon – Sat, 10am – 5pm, Sun, 2.30 to 6pm. *(F)*

Cabinet War Rooms, King Charles Street: 0171-930-6961. Daily 10am to 6pm (off Whitehall) *(C)*

Chelsea Physic Garden: 0171-352-5646, Wednesday & Sunday, 2pm to 5pm. *(C)*

Courtauld Institute Galleries, Somerset House: 0171-873-2526. Mon – Sat, 10am to 6pm, Sunday 2pm to 6pm. Last entry half an hour before closing time. *(C)*

Covent Garden (information on events): 0171-836-9136, Daily 10am to 6pm. *(C)*

Dickens House Museum: 48, Doughty Street: 0171-405-2127, Mon – Sat, 10am to 5pm. Closed Sundays and Bank Holidays. *(C)*

Guildhall, City of London: 0171-606-3030, daily 10am to 5pm (May to September); Mon – Sat 10am to 5pm (October to April) *(F)*

Appendix C: General Information

HMS *Belfast*, Symons Wharf, Vine Lane: 0171-407-6434; Daily, 11am to 5.50pm (Summer); Daily, 11am to 4.30pm (Winter). *(C)*

Imperial War Museum, Lambeth Road: 0171-416-5000, Mon – Sun 10am to 6pm *(C)*

London Transport Museum, Covent Garden: 0171-836-8557; Daily, 10am to 6pm. *(C)*

Museum of London, London Wall: 0171-600-3699; Tue – Sat, 10am to 5.30pm; Sun, Noon to 5.30pm. *(C)*

National Army Museum, Royal Hospital Road: 0171-730-0717; Daily 10am to 5.30pm. *(C)*

National Gallery, Trafalgar Square: 0171-839-3321; Mon – Sat, 10am to 6pm; Sun, 2pm to 6pm. *(F)*

National Portrait Gallery, St Martin's Place: 0171-306-0055; Mon – Sat, 10am to 6pm; Sun, noon to 6pm. *(F)*

Natural History Museum, Cromwell Road: 0171-938-9123; Mon – Sat, 10am to 5.50pm; Sun, 11am to 5.50pm. *(C)*

Regent's Park Zoo, Regent's Park: 0171-722-3333; Daily, 10am to 5.30pm. *(C)*

Royal Hospital, Royal Hospital Road, SW3: 0171-730-0161; Mon – Sat, times vary. *(F)* – though it is usual to tip the In-Pensioner for "services rendered".

Science Museum, Exhibition Road: 0171-938-8008; Mon – Sat, 10am to 6pm; Sun, 11am to 6pm. *(C)*

Tate Gallery, Millbank: 0171-887-8000; Mon – Sat, 10am to 5.50pm; Sun, 2pm to 5.50pm. *(F)*

Thames Barrier Visitors' Centre, Unity Way: 0181-854-1373; weekdays 10am to 5pm, weekends 10.30am to 5.30pm. *(C)*

Tower Bridge: 0171-378-1928; daily, 10am to 6pm. *(C)*

Tower of London, Tower Hill: 0171-709-0765; Mon – Sat, 9am – 6pm; Sun, 10am to 6pm. *(C)*

Victoria and Albert Museum, Cromwell Road: 0171-938-8500; Tues – Sun, 10am to 5.50pm; Mon, 12.00 – 5.50pm. *(C)*

War Cabinet Rooms, Clive Steps, King Charles Street, SW1: 0171-930-6961; daily 10am to 6pm. *(C)*

Churches

Opening and service times vary throughout London, many having to be kept locked when there are no "church-watchers" on duty. A simple telephone call could save a wasted journey.

All Hallows by the Tower: 0171-488-4772

Grosvenor Chapel: 0171-499-1684

St Clement Danes: 0171-242-8282

St George's Cathedral: 0171-928-5256

St Giles in the Fields: 0171-240-2532

St John's Wood Church: 0171-586-3864

St Martin in the Fields: 0171-930-1862

St Mary le Strand: 0171-836-3126

St Paul's Cathedral, Chapter House: 0171-236-4128

St Paul Covent Garden: 0171-836-5221

Savoy Chapel: 0171-836-7221

Westminster Abbey: 0171-222-5152

Westminster Cathedral: 0171-834-7452

Appendix D: Researching Family History

For visitors wishing to research their family history the following organisations hold substantial records. It may be necessary to visit more than one in order to obtain a complete record.

St Catherine's House, 10 Kingsway, WC2. The office of the Registrar General of births, deaths and marriages registered in England and Wales since 1st July 1837. Before that time parish registers were the only official record of these events.

Public Record Office, Chancery Lane, WC2; 0181-876-3444. Houses the Census Returns from 1841 to 1901 and is chief repository of the state archives of England. It also has a small, but interesting, museum that is open to the public Monday to Friday 1pm to 4pm. Modern documents are stored at Kew, off Mortlake Road.

Greater London Record Office, 40 Northampton Road, EC1; 0171-332-3820. Here are stored the parish records of London prior to July 1837, together with a reference library on London and its environs. Numerous parish records from the Diocese of London have been deposited here for safe keeping.

Guildhall Library, City of London; 0171-606-3030. In addition to housing the finest collection of books on London, the manuscripts department has a comprehensive collection of City of London parochial records. There is also a prints and maps department.

Most public libraries have reference sections and these often have information on local places and people.

Appendix E: Visitorcall – The Phone Guide To London

London Tourist Board operates a comprehensive range of recorded information services which are available 24 hours a day. *Visitorcall* is more than just a talking guidebook. It's updated daily to give you the latest information on exhibitions, theatres, concerts, places to visit, sightseeing, pageantry and much more. Simply dial 0839 123 followed by the three numbers shown below for each subject (calls cost 49p/minute at all times and are only accessible within the UK); to order free cards listing all services call 0171-971-0026:

What's On?

What's on this week	400	Current Exhibitions	403
What's On – next 3 months	401	Rock & Pop Concerts	422
Sunday in London	407	Lord Mayor's Show	
Summer in the Parks	406	State Opening of Parliament	
Christmas/Easter Events	418	& Trooping The Colour	413
Changing The Guard	411		

THEATRE

Popular West End Shows	416	New Productions/How to book	438
Beyond the West End	434		

PLACES TO VISIT

Popular Attractions	480	Greenwich/Military Museums	482
Museums	429	Famous Houses & Gardens	483
Palaces (inc Buckingham Pal)	481	Day Trips from London	484

Where To Take The Children

What's on	404	Places to visit	424

Out & About

Getting around London	430	Getting to the Airports	433
River Trips/Boat Hire	432	Shopping in London	486
Guided Tours/Walks	431	Street Markets	428
How to book a Guide/		Pubs, Restaurants &	
Bespoke Guided Tours	420	Afternoon Teas	485

ACCOMMODATION

WEATHER

General Advice	435	Met Office Forecast for	
Bookings Hotline	0171-824-8844	Greater London	0839-500-951

Appendix F: Tourist Information Offices

Personal Callers Only

British Travel Centre: 12, Regent Street, Piccadilly, London SW1Y 4PQ

City of London Information Centre: St Paul's Churchyard South, London EC4.

Liverpool Street: Liverpool Street Underground Station, London EC2M 7PN

Selfridges: Selfridges Store, Basement Services Arcade, Oxford Street, London W1

Southwark: Hay's Galleria, Tooley Street, London SE1 2HD

Victoria: Victoria Station Forecourt, London SW1V 1JU

Waterloo: London Visitor Centre, Arrivals Hall, Waterloo International Terminal, London SE1 7LT

Source: Tourist Information Centres in England 1995/96; Published by the English Tourist Board. 1995.

Index

Abbreviations used: highw = highwayman; histn = historian; refrm = reformer; surgn = surgeon

A

Abbeys
  Barking, 132
  Bermondsey, 9
  Dominican Priory(Catholic), 104
  Kilburn Abbey, 90
  St Mary of Bethlehem, 68
  Westminster, 24-25, 35, 95-97, 146
Acheson, Edward Goodrich, 126
"Achilles", 87
Acton Road, The, 73
Actors/Actresses
  Fields, Gracie, 93
  Garrick, David, 102
  Gielgud, Sir John, 61
  Hicks (nee Terry), 78, 79
  Hicks, Sir Seymour, 78, 79
  Irving, Sir Henry, 78, 102
  Kean, Edmund, 42
  Novello, Ivor, 79
  Olivier, Lord Laurence, 7
  Shakespeare, Edmund, 147
  Siddons, Sarah, 89
  Terry, Ellen, 38, 78
  Warner, Jack, 88
  Wolfit, Sir Donald, 79
Actors Church Union, 38
Acts of Parliament
  Church Building Act (1818), 67
  Dissolution of Monasteries (1539), 58
  Fifty New Churches (1771), 130, 132, 133
  National Theatre Act (1949), 6
Admiralty, 31
  Arch, 34, 102
  House, former, 30, 100-101
Agar Town, King's Cross, 112
Albany, Piccadilly, 62
Albert Bridge Company, 120
Albert Memorial, 68
Aldwych, 1
Alexander Fleming House, 8
American Civil War, 104
Angel of Christian Charity, 76
"Apostle of Free Trade", 104
Apsley House, 13, 86, 143
Arch of Constantine, 12
Architects
  Adam, Robert, 12, 13, 30, 87, 101, 105, 124
  Archer and Green, 64
  Architects Co-Partnership, 52
  Atkinson, R.F., 75
  Baker, Sir Herbert, 40
  Balfour and Turner, 40
  Barlow, W.H., 112
  Barry, Sir Charles, 38, 114
  Bauhaus Movement, 92, 122
  Bedford, Francis, 6, 19
  Bennet, Sir Hubert, 6
  Bentley, John Francis, 22
  Blomfield, Sir Arthur, 68
  Burnham, Daniel, 75
  Burton, Decimus, 86
  Chambers, Sir William, 4
  Chapman Taylor and Partners, 23
  Colcutt, T., 42
  Comper, Sir Ninian, 140
  Corbett, Harvey W., 1
  Cubitt. Thomas, 18, 68, 119, 134
  Dance, George, 57
  de Syllas, Leo, 5
  Donaldson, T.L., 67
  Drake, Lindsey, 122
  Edmiston, J & J.S., 122
  Edwin, Richard, 75
  Emberton, Joseph, 62
  Emden, Walter, 102
  Fontana, Carl, 3
  Fowke, Francis, 68, 69
  Fowler, Sir John, 38, 117
  Francis, Frederick, 90
  Francis, Horace, 90
  Gibberd, Frederick, 126
  Gibbs, James, 2, 41, 43, 79
  Gibson, J.S., 98
  Goldfinger, Erno, 8
  Green, William Curtis, 12
  Gribble, Herbert, 67
  Hardwicke, Philip, 121, 126
  Hawksmoor, Nicholas, 130, 132, 133
  Hurst, Aaron, 112
  Inwood, Henry, 11
  Johnson, Frederick, 134
  Jones, Inigo, 4, 38
  Kent, William, 30
  Lasdun, Sir Denis, 5, 122
  Lewis Solomons, Kaye and Partners, 13
  Lidbetter, Hubert, 110
  Lutyens, Sir Edwin, 29
  Mackenzie, A.G.R., 2
  Mackenzie, Marshall, 2
  Martin, J.L., 6
  Matthew, Sir Robert, 6, 76
  Mewes and Davis, 63
  Nash, John, 12, 34, 40, 61, 73, 75, 109
  Novosielski, Michael, 61
  Paxton, Sir Joseph, 67
  Phipps, C.J., 60, 61, 76, 102
  Pugin,
    Edward Welby, 90
    August Welby Northmore, 10, 90
  Richard Seifert & Partners, 59, 103
  Ripley, Thomas, 30, 101

Index

Schaufelberg, Ernest, 39, 78
Scott,
  A.T., 40
  George Gilbert, 68, 97, 112, 114
  Giles Gilbert, 4, 60, 103
  John Oldrid, 140
Shaw, John, 44
Smith, S.J.R., 146
Soane, Sir John, 6
Sprague, W.G.R., 79, 102
Stevens and Munt, 65
Street, George Edmund, 14, 19, 79
Talman, John, 3
Tasker, John, 108
Taylor, J. H., 70
Terry Quinlan Partnership, 78
Tite, Sir William, 17
Vulliamy, Lewis, 107
Wallis Gilbert & Partners, 117
Waterhouse, Alfred, 68
Webb, Sir Aston, 34, 102
Wilkin, William n
Wren, Sir Christopher, 2, 43, 44, 53, 79, 101
Wyatt, Benjamin Dean, 40
Art Galleries
  Angerstein, John Julius, 77
  Clore Gallery, 147
  Courtauld Institute of Art, Strand, 4
  National Gallery, 101
  National Portrait, 31, 102
  Royal Academy of Art, 63, 151
  Tate, Millbank, 14, 77, 146
Artari and Bagutti (plasterers), 78
Artists
  Camden Town Artists, 104
  Cotman, John Sell, 126
  Feibusch, Hans, 6
  Gainsborough, Thomas, 63, 102
  Hayden, Benjamin Robert, 89
  Reynolds, Sir Joshua, 63
  Sandby, Paul, 63
  Sickert, W.R., 104
  West, Benjamin, 63
Ashurst House, 107
Australia House, 2, 41
Authors
  Beeton, Mrs, 17
  Beast, William, 9
  Borrow, George, 69
  Collins, Wilkie, 125
  Conan Doyle, Sir Arthur, 11, 12, 34
  Dickens, Charles, 37, 125
  Forster, John, 7
  Hardy, Thomas, 90
  Mander, Raymond, 102
  Mitchenson, Joe, 102
  Sala, George Augustus, 112
  Stow, John, 114
  Thackeray, William Makepeace, 69
  Wallace, Edgar, 81

B

BBC, 1, 41
Baden-Powell, Lord, 68
Bailey, Lillian, 6
Baker Street, 11
Bank of England, 53, 150
Barretts of Wimpole Street, 125
Battle Bridge, 112
Belgravia, 85, 119
Benedictine Convent, Bayswater, 73
"Bible in Spain", 69
"Big Bang", 57
Bishops and Archbishops
  Archbishops,
    Canterbury,
      (Randell Thomas Davidson), 139
  Bishops,
    London, (William Wand), 48
    Southwark, (Edward Talbot), 139
    Winchester,
      (William of Wykeham), 138
      (William Gifford), 139
Blackwall Tunnel, 130
"Blue Lamp" The, 88
"Blues". The, 69
"Boatswain", 87
"Bobbies", 9
Bonnie Prince Charles, 3
Booth, General and Mrs William, 115
Bow Street Magistrates; Court, 40
Brennikmeyers Family, 74
Brettenham House, 4
Bricklayers Arms, 10
Bridges
  Albert, 120
  Blackfriars, 7
  Lambeth, 15
  London, 7, 131
  Putney, 70
  Waterloo, 4, 7
  Westminster, 7, 93
Brigade of Guards, 30
Britain at War experience, 148
British & Foreign Bible Society, 69
British Travel Centre, 62
Brixton, 15
Broomfield, Elizabeth (builder), 119
Buckingham Palace Road, 14
Bunting, William, 69
Burlington, Earls of, 62
Burlington House, Piccadilly, 62
Bush House, 1, 41
Business Design Centre, 113
"By Appointment", 64

C

Cade, Jack (rebel), 82
Cadwalla, 44, 81
Cambridge Circus, 103
Camden,
  High Street, 104
  Lock, 104
Campbell-Bannerman, Sir Henry, 29
Canada Water, 9
Canary Wharf, 133
Canals
  Alexandra, 117

Grand Junction, 72, 89
Grand Union, 73, 133
Limehouse Basin, 133
Paddington Basin, 72
Regent Canal, 89, 104
Candlewick Street, 81
Cannon Street, 81
Cantiacorium (Canterbury), 88
Captain Blood, 23, 95
Cardinals
  Beaufort, 137, 138
  Bourne, 105
  Vaughan, 22, 93
  Wiseman, 105
Cathedrals
  St. George's Catholic, 10
  St. Paul's, 44, 47, 81, 150
    Choir School (new), 52, 81
    Choir School (old), 53
    Plans, 50
  Southwark, 136, 147
    Harvard Chapel, 137
    Gwilt's tomb, 137
    Plan, 136
    Shakespeare Memorial Window, 141
  Westminster (Catholic), 22, 93, 146
Catherine of Arragon & Castille, 7
Cemeteries
  Abney Park, Stoke Newington, 115
  Brompton, 69
  Highgate, 107
  South Metropolitan, 17
  West Norwood, 17
Cenotaph, Whitehall, 29, 98, 100
Central Hill, 19
Centre Point, 59, 103
Chalk Farm Road, 104
Channel Tunnel, 74
Chapel Royal of France, former, 125
Charing Cross Road, 78
Charles I, 4, 29
Chelsea,
  Barracks, 119
  Football Club, 69
  Royal Hospital, 119
Cheshunt, Herts., 80
Chinatown, 60
Church of England's Council on
  Foreign Affairs, 44, 80
Churchill, Lord Randolph, 88
Churchill, Sir Winston, 4, 88
Churches
  American Church, 104
  Brompton Oratory, 65
  Christ Church,
    Cubitt Town, 134
    Victoria Street, 23
  Crown Court, Covent Garden, 39
  German, Forest Hill, 17
  Norwegian (St Olave), 10
  Orange Street Congregational, 34
  Our Lady of the Rosary & St Dominic, 104
  Orthodox Churches, 44, 80
  Royal Air Force Central, 2, 41, 43
  Sacred Heart of Jesus, Kilburn, 90

All Hallows-by-the-Tower, 82, 132
All Hallows the Great, Upper Thames St, 57
All Saints, Fulham, 70
Holy Trinity Brompton (HTB), 65, 67
St. Alphege, Greenwich, 129-130
St. Andrew Holborn, 105
St. Anne, Limehouse, 133
St. Augustine, Watling Street, 53
St. Barnabas, Victoria, 119
St. Bride, Fleet Street, 44, t31
St. Clement Danes, Strand, 2, 41, 43, 79
St Clement Eastcheap, 43, 56
St. Dunstan-in-the West, Fleet Street, 44, 80
St. George-in-the-East, 132
St. Giles-in-the-Fields, 110
St. James Chapel, Pentonville Road, 112
St. James, Piccadilly, 62
St. James the Less, Vauxhall Bridge Road, 14
St. John, Walham Green, 70
St. John, Waterloo Road, 6
St. John's Wood Church, 126
St. Joseph, Highgate, 108
St. Luke, West Norwood, 15, 19
St. Margaret, Lothbury, 57
St. Margaret Pattens, 83, 131
St. Margaret, Westminster, 24-35
St. Martin-in-the-Fields, 31, 78
St. Martin-within-Ludgate, 44, 81
St. Mary Aldermary, 53
St. Mary with All Souls, Kilburn, 90
St. Mary at Hill, 17
St. Mary in the Fields, Kilburn, 90
St. Mary Le Bow, Cheapside, 10S
St. Mary Le Strand, 2, 41
St. Mary-on-Paddington-Green, 89
St. Mary, Putney, 70
St. Mary (old), Stoke Newington, 114
St. Mary Woolnoth, City, 56
St. Matthew, Brixton, 15
St. Michael,
  Cornhill, City, 56
  Highgate, 107
  Ladbroke Grove, 122
St. Pancras "New" church, 111
St. Paul, Covent Garden, 38
St. Peter-upon-Cornhill, City, 56
St. Servatius, Maastricht, Belgium, 67
St. Stephen, Walbrook, City, 57
City of London Club, 58
City of London Information Centre, 81
Clayton, The Rev'd "Tubby", 82, 132
Clissold, The Rev'd Augustus, 114
Coade Artificial Stone Manufactory, 113
Coade, Eleanor, 113
Coade Stone, 112
Cochrane's Revues, 78
Cole, Sir Henry, 69
Colin, Pere, 70
Collins, Sam, 113
Confederation of British Industry (CBI), 103
"Confessions of St Augustine", 139
Connaught Place, 88
Cons, Emma, 6
"Conservation in Action", 128
Constantine Arch, Rome, 109

Index

Convent of the Belgravians", 1 IS)
Conway House, Kilburn, 90
"Copenhagen"(horse), 13
Copperfield, David, 7
Cornhill Magazine, 69
Covent Garden, 38
Cow, Henry, 17
Cricket Mecca, 89
Crimean War, 104
Crimean War & Indian Mutiny Memorial, 97
Croatia, Miss, 114
Cromwell, Oliver, 4, 30
Cromwell House, Highgate, 107
Cromwell Road, 5
Crown Jewels of England, 83
Crystal Palace, 11, 19
  Football Club, 19
  Parade, 19
Cubitt, William (Builder), 134
Cutlers, Worshipful Company of, 7

D

Damer, Joseph, Earl of Dorchester, 12
"David", 13, 64, 86
David Copperfield Gardens, 8
"David Garrick", 102
Davy Safety Lamp for miners, 128
Davy, Sir Humphrey, 128
Dents (clockmakers), 112
Deva (Chester), 88
Devereux, Robert, Earl of Essex, 113
"Division Bell", 23
"Dorothy", 60
Doulton, Henry, 17
Dover Stage, 7
Downing,
  Sir George, 29, 98, 100
  Street, 29, 100
D'Oyly Carte, Richard, 60
"Dragon", 80
Druids, Ancient Order of, 127
Drury Lane, 40
Dubris (Dover), 88
Duchy of Lancaster, 4
Duncannon Street, 30

E

East India Company, 75
Ebury Street, 119
Edgware Road, 88
Effra Road, 15
Eisenhower, General Dwight, 13
Eleanor Cross, 35, 78
Elephant and Castle, 7
Elf Aquitaine UK, 84
"Endemion", 105
Engineers
  Bazalgette, Sir Joseph, 70, 120
  Brunel, Isambard Kingdom, 121
  Dodd, George, 4
  Fitzmaurice, Sir Maurice, 10
  Hawkshaw, John, 35
  Jones, Sir Horace, 43
  Morgan, Sir Charles, 117

Ordish, R.C., 112, 120
Rennie, John, 4
Trevithick, Richard, 111
English Channel (Tunnel), 74
English Civil War Society, 101
"Eros", 76, 151
Eton College, 127
Erechtheion, Athens, 111
Euston Road, 110

F

Falmoulh Road, 8
"Far from the Madding Crowd", 90
Faraday, Michael (inventor)8
Ferdinand of Spain, 24
Ferdinand Road, 104
Festival of Britain (1951), 5, 6
Fleming, Alexander (scientist), 8, 72
Fleet,
  Road, 105
  Street, 7, 44
  Prince Henry's Room, 44
Fortnum, William, 62
Fountain Court, 43
Fox, George, 109
Foyle,
  Gilbert, 59
  William, 59
Franklin, Benjamin, 34
French Embassy, Knightsbridge, 64
French Free Forces, Dorset Square, 125
Friends House, 110
Frith, Mary alias "Moll Cutpurse"
  (pickpocket), 44
Fulham,
  Broadway, 69
  Football Club(Chelsea), 69

G

Galleywall Road, 9
Gascoyne, Sir Crisp, 53
Gielgud, Sir John (actor), 61
Gloucester House, Park Lane, 12
"God save the Duke", 4
Goldley, John Robert, 125
Gordon Rioters, 7
Grange Road, 9
Great Exhibition (of, 1851), 18, 67, 112
  clock at King's Cross, 112
Great Fire (of, 1666), 44
Great Plague (of, 1665), 23
Greek Community, Brotherhood of, 17
Grocers, Worshipful Company of, 54
Grosvenor,
  Baron, 117
  Gardens, 114
  Robert, 12
Grove, The, 107
Grove, George, 68
Guildhall (London), 150
Gwynne, Nell, 40

H

HMS Belfast, 148
HMS Crystal Palace, 19
HMS Victory, 77
H.T.B (Holy Trinity Brompton), 67
Hamley, William, 75
Hampstead Lane, 105
Hard Rock Cafe, Piccadilly, 63
Harrods, Henry Charles, 65
Harrow Road Police Station, 88
Harvard, John, 137
Harvard College, USA, 100
Hippodrome, 122
Hitler, Adolf, 122
Holmes, Sherlock, 11
Holmhurst St Mary, East Sussex, 45
Holt, Richard, 113
Holy Name of Mary,
  Convent, 70
  Sisters of, 70
Horse Guards Parade, 30, 100, 101
"Horse of Helios" - the Sun God, 60, 76
"Horses of the Sun", 2

Hospitals
  Broadmoor, Crowthorne, Berks., 58
  Elizabeth Garrett Anderson, Euston Road, 111
  London Smallpox, 112
  Mildmay, 114
  St. George's Tooting, 64
  St. Mary's, Praed Street, Paddington, 72
  St. Olave's, 9
  Royal Bethlem, 7, 10, 58
  Royal Free, 105
  Westminster Infirmary, 86

Hotels
  Bath, Piccadilly, 63
  Carlton, Haymarket, 76
  Churchill, Portman Square, 124
  Dorchester, Park Lane, 12, 14
  Gordon Hotels Ltd, 12
  Great Western Royal, Praed Street, 121
  Grosvenor, Victoria, 117
  Grosvenor House, Park Lane, 12
  Hyde Park, Knightsbridge, 64
  Lanesborough, Hyde Park Corner, 64, 86
  London Hilton, Park Lane, 13
  Metropole, Edgware Road, 88
  Paris Ritz, 63
  Portman Inter-Continental,
    Portman Square, 124
  Ritz., Piccadilly, 63
  Savoy, 42
  St Pancras Station, 112
  Waldorf, Aldwych, 79
Houdah, 7
Houses of Parliament, 14, 25, 146
Household Cavalry, 30

Housing
  Hallfield Estate, Bishop's Bridge Road, 121
  Lillingston Estate, Vauxhall Bridge Road, 14
  Trellick Tower, Golbourne Road, 123
Howland Great Wet Dock, 9
Hussars, 3rd, 86
Hyde Park Corner, 64, 86

I

"Ich Dien" - "I Serve", 44, 80
India House, Aldwych, 40
"Indian Queen", 40
Infanta of Castille, 7
Inniskilling Dragoons, 13, 86

Inns and Taverns
  Albert, Victoria Street, 23, 93
  Cherry Garden, Bermondsey, 10
  Cock, Kilburn High Road, 90
  Coal Hole, Strand, 42
  Crown Tavern, former, Russell Street, 35
  Cubitt Arms, Docklands, 134
  Flask, Highgate, 107
  Fountain Tavern, Strand, 42
  George, Strand, 3
  Green Man, Putney Heath, 71
  Hand and Racquet, Whitcombe Street, 34
  Lansdowne Arms, Islington, 113
  Jamaica, Jamaica Road, 10
  King's Head, Fulham High Street, 70
  Old Queen's Head, Islington, 113
  Queen's Elm, Fulham, 69
  Queen's Tree, Fulham, 69
  Sherlock Homes,
    Northumberland Avenue, 34
  Spaniards, Hampstead, 106
  Thurlow Arms, West Norwood, 15
  Two Chairmen, Warwvick House Street, 34
  Victoria, Woolwich Road, Charlton, 130
  White Swan, Crystal Palace Parade, 19
  Windsor Castle, Park Road, 126
Institute of the Oratory (Oratorians), 65
Irish Church Hostels Company, 90
"Iron Duke", 86
Isabella of Spain, 24
"Ivanhoe", 60, 103

J

Jamaica Road, 10
Jockey Club, 64
"Joy of Life", 87
"Jude the Obscure", 90

K

Keats,
  Grove, 105
  House, 105
Kenwood House, 105
Kilburn High Road, 89
Killigrew, Thomas, 40
King'sArmy, 101
King's College, London, 3, 41, 126
King's Company, 40
King's Highway, 73
King's Mere pond, 70
"King's Rhapsody", 60
King's Royal Rifle Corps, 85
King's Troop Royal Horse Artillery, 109
Knightsbridge Green, 64

Index

L

Lambeth,
  Borough of, 15
  Marsh, 6
  Road, 7
  Town Hall, 15
Lancaster Place, 4
Lane, James, 2nd Viscount Lanesborough, 86
Lauderdale House, Highgate, 107
"Les Miserables", 60
Leslie, Henry J., 60
"Letters of Appointment", 63
Lewis,
  John, 74
  John Spedan, 72
Libraries
  British Library (new), 111
  Cambridge University, 111
  Central Reference Library (Westminster), 34
  Copyright Libraries, 111
  National Library of Scotland, 111
  National Library of Wales, 111
  National Newspaper Library, Colindale, 111
  Oxford University (Bodlien Library), 111
  Trinity College, Dublin, 111
Lisson Grove, 89
"Little Ben", Victoria, 14, 84
Little Venice, 89, 104
Lloyds Bank, Edgware Road, 88
Londinium (London), 82, 88
London Central Mosque, Regent's Park, 136
London Docklands
  Development Corporation, 133
London Dungeon, 148
London Football Club, 69
London Pavilion, 76
London Stone, 82
London Tourist Board, 85
London Trained (Train) Band, 107
London Zoological Gardens, 124, 126
Lord, Thomas, 89, 125
Lord's Cricket Ground, 89, 125, 126
"Loves of Ergas", The, 61
Lower Marsh Road, 7
Lund, Giusseppe (designer), 87

M

MCC, 89
M.I.5 & M.I.6 headquarters, 14
Machine Gun Corps, 14, 64, 86
Madam Tussaud's Rock Circus, 76
Magna Carta, 98
Mansion House, 53, 57
Maps
  Aldwych, 36
  Bank, 55
  Chelsea, 118
  Covent Garden, 36
  Crystal Palace Park, 21
  Highgate, 106
  Kilburn, 91
  Norwood Cemetery, 18
  Parliament Square, 26
  South Kensington (museums), 66
  Tourist Attractions, 144-145
  Trafalgar Square, 32
  West Norwood, 16
  Whitehall, 99
Marble Arch, 12, 73, 88, 109, 143
Markets
  Hungerford, Charing Cross, 35
  Portman, Marylebone, 89
  Smithfield, 110
Marks & Spencer's Baker Street, 12
Marsden, William (surgn), 18, 105
Marshalsea Prison, 7
Marylebone,
  Cricket Club (MCC), 89, 125
  Flyover, 88
Mason, Hugh, 62
McAlpine, Sir Robert, 12
"Me and my girl", 85
"Meet me Victoria", 85
Mercers, Worshipful Company of, 54
Merchant Taylors' Hall, 56
Messel, Oliver (interior designer), 13
Methodist Central Hall, Westminster, 97
Metropolitan Tabernacle, 8
Meux Family, 80
Meuxs's Horse Shoe Brewery, 103
Michelham, Lord, 13
Middlesex,
  Forest, 114
  Guildhall, former, 25, 98
Midland Clock Works, Derby, 84
Mildmay House, 114
Mile Stone, 73, 82
Ministry of Defence, 30
Mithraic Temple, 53, 57
Monarchy
  Anne, 3, 45, 61
  Arthur(Prince), 7, 20, 24
  Boudicea of the Iceni, 112
  Canute, 2
  Catherine of Arragon & Castille, 7
  Charlotte, 199
  Charlotte(Princess), 6
  Edward the Confessor, 24
  Edward I, 1, 35, 78, 80
  Edward VI, 4
  Edward VII, 68, 140
  Eleanor of Castille, 35, 78
  Elizabeth I, 15, 113
  Elizabeth II, 76, 878, 131
  Elizabeth, Queen Mother, 5, 15, 87
  George II, 29
  George III, 63, 119
  George IV, 12, 105, 109
  George V, 15
  Harold Harefoot, 2
  Henrietta Maria, 4
  Henry, (Prince), 44, 80
  Henry I, 140
  Henry V, 1138
  Henry V1124
  Henry VIII, 7, 78
  John, 98
  John of Gaunt, 137, 138
  Leopold(Prince), 6

Mary, 15
Richard II, 136
Robert of Gloucester, 81
Rufus, 146
Sigbert, 96, 146
Victoria I, 20, 47, 64.68
William the Conqueror, 146
William IV, 131
Monument, The, 57, 148
"Moonstone", 125
Moriarty, Doctor, 35
"Morning Herald", 8
Morrison, Herbert, 4
Mozart family, 119
Mudchute Farm, Docklands, 135
Museums
  Alexander Fleming, Praed Street, 72
  Apsley House, Hyde Park Corner, 13, 86
  Baden-Powell House, Kensington, 68
  Bank of England, City, 56
  "Black Museum" New Scotland Yard, 24
  British, Great Russell Street, 110
  Dickens House. Doughty Street
  Fine and Applied Arts, 67
  Geological, Kensington, 68
  Imperial War, Lambeth, 7, 10, 58
  HMS Belfast, 148
  War Cabinet Rooms, 29, 98
  London Transport, Covent Garden, 38
  National Maritime, Greenwich, 130
  Royal Hospital, Chelsea, 119
  St Bride's Church, Fleet Street, 81
  Science, Kensington, 68, 110
  Soane, Lincoln's Inn Fields, 6
  Theatre, Covent Garden, 39
  Victoria and Albert, Kensington, 5, 65, 67-68
  Wallace Collection, Manchester Square, 75
Myddelton, Sir Hugh, 113

N

"No., 1 London", 87
Napolean III, 64, 104
Nash Terraces, 125
"National Cruet Set", 31, 102
National Theatre Company, 5, 7
NatWest Tower, 58
Nelson, Horatio, Lord, 12, 109
New Kent Road, 8
New River,
  Company, 113
  Upper Reservoir, 113
New Road, The, 73, 111
New Zealand,
  High Commission, 76
  House, 76
Newgate prison, 73
Newington Green, 114
Newton, Sir Isaac, 34
Nine Elms, Vauxhall, 38
"No Popery", 7
"Noah's Ark", Holborn, 75
North China Bank, 82
North Kensington Fire Station,
  Ladbroke Road, 122

Norwich School of Painting, 126
Norwood,
  High Street, 19
  Road, 15

O

Oblates of Mary Immaculate, Order of, 90
"Ode on a Grecian Urn", 105
"Ode to a Nightingale", 105
"Ode to Autumn", 105
Open Spaces (Public)
  Hampstead Heath, 105
  Ponds, 105
  Parliament Hill Fields, 105
  Primrose Hill, 126-127
  Putney Heath, 70
  Ranelagh Gardens, 120
  Wimbledon Common, 70
"Oranges and Lemons", 43, 79
Orchard Portman, Somerset, 12
Orchard Street, 12
Oriental Club, 75
Our Lady of Kilburn (shrine), 90
Owen, Prof. Richard, 20
Oxford and Cambridge Boat Race, 70
Oxford,
  Circus, 76
  Movement, 90
  Road, 73
  Street, 12, 73, 109

P

Paddington, 72
  Green, 72
  Green Police Station, 88
Palaces
  Buckingham, 12, 14, 63, 85, 143
  Fulham, 70
    The Warren, 70
  Greenwich, Queens' House, 130
  Hampton Court, Grand Hall, 98
  St. James, 31, 63
  Savoy, 42
    Chapel, 4, 42
  Whitehall, Banqueting House, 29, 100-101
Palmer, H.E., 2
Paragon Gardens, 10
Park Lane, 13
Parks
  Battersea, 120
  Bermondsey (Spa), 9
  Clissold, Stoke Newington, 114
  Dinosaur Theme Park, Crystal Palace, 19-30
  Geraldine Mary Harmsworth, 10
  Gordon's, Chicago, 25
  Green, 63
  Hyde, 12, 64
    Rotten Row, 64
    Speakers' Corner, 87
  Norwood, 19
  Regent's Zoo, 124-126
  Southwark, 9
  Waterlow, Highgate, 107

Index

Parliament,
  Square, 98
  Street, 98
Passion of Jesus Christ, (the Passionists), Congregation of, 108
Patten, William, 114
Pattins, 82
Peel, Sir Robert, 58
"Peelers", 27
Penn, William, 111
Pennsylvania, Colony of
Petanque or Boule, 127
Pentonville
  Estate, 112
  Road, 112
"Peppercorn Rent", 68, 114
Pepys, Samuel (diarist), 10, 44, 80, 107
Pere Colin, 79
Petty France, 86
"Petticoat Lane", 83
Pevsner, Prof., Sir Nikolaus, 6, 112, 117
Piccadilly House, 62
Piccadilly, 62
  Circus, 76
Pimlico Road, 119
Pius IX, Pope, 22
Plans
  St Paul's Cathedral, 50
  Southwark Cathedral, 136
  Westminster Abbey, 94
Playwrights
  Albery, James, 78
  Pitt, Archie, 93
  Robertson, T.W., 102
  Shakespeare, William, 6., 137
  Travers, Ben, 79
  Vanburgh, Sir John, 61
  Wilde, Oscar, 61
Poets
  Coleridge, Samuel Taylor, 107
  Cowper, William, 80
  Dryden, John, 40
  Gower, John, 136, 139
  Keats, John, 105
  Lovelace, Robert, 44
  Swinburne, Algernon, 70
  Watts-Dunton, Theodore, 70
Pool of London, 10
Poperinghe, near Ypres, Belgium, 83, 132
Porden, William, 15
Porter, John (builder), 61
Portman,
  Estate, 12
  Henry, 12
Praed
  Street, 72
  William, 72
Prince Henry's Room, Fleet Street, 44, 80
Propriety Chapel, 13
Putney,
  Bridge Approach (road), 70
  Hill, 70

Q

Quadriga, Wellington Arch, 13, 86
Quaker Movement, 110, 111
Queen Elizabeth I College, Greenwich, 129
Queen Elizabeth II Conference Centre, 24, 97
Queen Mother Sports Centre, 14
Quex Road, Kilburn, 90

R

Raffles, Sir Stamford, 127
"Railway Hudson", 64
Railway Companies (former)
  Great Western, 121
  London and Birmingham, 111
  London and South Western, 6
  London, Chatham and Dover, 117
  Midland, 112
  South Eastern, 35, 57
Ranelagh, Lord, 120
Remembrance Sunday, 3, 9
Restoration of the Monarchy, (1660), 30
Richie, Archibald (builder), 67
"Ritzy", 63
Rivers
  Effra, 15
  Fleet, 44, 105
  Rhine, 5
  Stamford Brook, 69
  Tyburn, 3, 4, 63, 74, 110
Rivett, Mr. (blacksmith), 30
Rock Island Diner, 76
"Rock of Ages", 34
Rogers, Prebendary John, 139
Roman London
  "Bath", 41
  Temple of Apollo, 24
  Temple of Diana, 81
  Temple of Mithras, 53, 57
  Villa, 83
"Romany Rye", The, 69
Rood Lane, 131
Rosebery Avenue, 7
Rothschild, Baron Nathan de, 58
Rotherhithe New Road, 9
Rotherhithe Tunnel, 10
Rothermere, Lord, 19
Royal Academy of Dramatic Art (RADA), 61
Royal Agricultural Hall, Islington, 113
Royal Albert Hall, 64
Royal College of Art, 68
Royal College of Music, 68
Royal College of Obstetricians & Gynaecologists, 126
Royal Courts of Justice, 43, 79, 150
  Chancery Division, 43
  Family Division, 43
  Queen's Bench Division, 43
Royal Exchange (Building), 17, 56
Royal Festival Hall, 6, 42, 147
Royal Foundation of St Katharine, 133
Royal Highlanders, 13, 86
Royal Institute of British Architects (RIBA), 108
Royal Pew, 31
Royal Regiment of Artillery, 13, 64, 86

Royal Shakespeare Company, 79
Royal Tennis Courts, 34
Royal Thames Yacht Club, Knightsbridge, 64
Royal Victorian Order, 42
Royal Welsh Fusiliers, 13, 86
Russian Baltic Fleet, 130
Russian Submarine, 130

S

Saint
  Ambrose, 140
  Augustine of Hippo, 140
  Basil the Great, 140
  Bridget, 81
  Clement, 2
  George and the Dragon, 97, 126
  George's,
    Circus, 7
    Fields, 7
    Road, 8
  Gregory Naziangen, 140
  James's Estate, 62
  Jerome, 140
  Justus, 139
  Katherine's,
    Dock, 132, 148
    House, 2
  Margaret of Antioch, 139
  Mary Magdalene, 132
  Mary of Barking, 132
  Olave of Norway, 138
  Peter, 139
  Philip Neri, 65
  Stephen's clock tower, 14
  Swithun, 139
  Thomas of Canterbury, 139
"Salad Days", 78
Salvation Army, 115
Samuel Pepys Club of London, 44, 80
Sanctuaries, 24
Sandell, Doctor, 119
Schools
  St Clement Danes CoE Primary, Drury Lane, 43
  St. Martin-in-the-Fields (Girls), 15
  St Mary CoE Primary, Kilburn, 90
  St Saviour & St Olave Grammar, Southwark, 8
  Virgo Fidelis (Catholic Girls), 19
  Westminster, 97
Scotland Yard - New, 95
Sculptors
  Bailey, E.H., 109
  Bainbridge, E.
  Belt, Charles, 87
  Bentham, P.J., 62
  Bird, Francis, 45
  Boehm, Edgar, 43
  Canova, 4
  Chantry, Sir Francis, 12
  Forster, Frank, 133
  Gibbons, Grinling, 101
  Gilbert, Alfred, 76
  Hoffman, Malvina, 41
  Huxley-Jones,
    Thomas, 81
  Jones, Adrian, 86
  Le Sueur, Hubert, 30, 101
  Mackennal, Bertram, 3
  Mallisard, G, 1
  Pearson, Lionel, 13
  Sargeant Jagger, 13
  Thomas, John, 113, 121
  Thorneycroft, Hamo, 2
  Weller, Rudy, 60, 76
  Westmacott, Richard, 87, 109
  Wood, Francis Derwent, 13, 64, 8
  Wynne, David, 87
Selfridge, Harry Gordon, 74
Shaftesbury, 7th Earl of, 76
Shaftesbury Memorial Fountain, 76
Shakespeare Memorial Window, 141
Sherlock Holmes, 11, 34, 35
  Hotel, 11
  Society, 11
Shops
  Aquascutum's, Regent Street, 76
  Army & Navy Store, Victoria, 93
  Burlington Arcade, 63
  C & A, Oxford Street, 74
  Camden Passage Islington(Antiques), 113
  Carnaby Street, Regent Street, 75
  Covent Garden, 38
  D.H. Evans, Oxford Street, 74
  Fortnum and Mason Ltd., Piccadilly, 62
  Foyle's Bookshop, Charing Cross Road, 59
  Hamley's Toy shop, Regent Street, 75
  Harrods, Brompton Road, 65
  John Lewis's, Oxford Street, 74
  Lilley & Skinner's, Oxford Street, 74
  Marks & Spencer's, Oxford Street, 74
  Peter Robinson's, Oxford Circus, 74
  Putney High Street, 70
  The Mall Arcade, Islington (Antiques), 113
  Selfridges, Oxford Street, 74
  Simpson's, Piccadilly, 62
  South Quays Shopping Centre, 9
"Show's the thing"., 93
Sigismund Goetz Fund, 87
Society of Mary, 70
Soho, 60
Somerset House, 4, 42, 51
Somme, Battle of, 13, 86
"Song of Norway", 60
"Sound of Music", 60
South Lambeth Road, 14
South Norwood Hill, 8
Southampton Road, 104
Southcott, Joanna, 126
Southwark, London Borough of, 8
Southwark Park Road, 9
Spurgeon, The Rev'd Charles, 8, 17
Squares
  Claremont, 11
  Dorset, 89
  Euston, 111
  Manchester, 75
  Portman, 12
  Trafalgar, 12, 711, 151
Stag Brewery, 93

Index

Stanhope,
  Earl (5th), 102
  Gate, 14
Star Street, 88
"Starlight Express", 92
Stations
British Rail
  Cannon Street, 57, 82
  Channel Tunnel, 6
  Charing Cross, 35, 78
  Euston, 11
  Kilburn High Road, 89
  King's Cross, 112
  Liverpool, 58
  Marylebone, 11, 85
  Nine Elms(Vauxhall), 6
  Paddington, 121
  Vauxhall, 14
  Victoria, 117, 143
  Waterloo, 6
  Wimbledon, 71
Stations
Docklands Light Railway
  Crossharbour, 134
  Island Gardens, 135
Underground
  Aldgate, 83
  Archway, 106
  Cannon Street, 57, 82
  Charing Cross, 35, 78
  Golders Green, 106
  Highgate, 106
  Knightsbridge, 64
  Marylebone, 89
  "Selfridges'", 74
  Surrey Quays, 9
  Wimbledon, 71
Statues
  Alanbrook, Viscount, 101
  Alfred the Great, 80
  Atlee, Lord Clement, 133
  Beaconsfield, Lord (Benjamin Disraeli), 27
  Byron, Lord George, 87
  Canning, George, 27
  Cavell, Nurse Edith, 3, 102
  Charles I, 30, 100-101
  Christ, 80
  Churchill, Sir Winston Spencer, 27
  Cobden, Richard, 104
  Derby, Lord, 27
  (Edward Geoffrey Smith Stanley) Dowding, Lord, 2
  Foch, Marshal, 14, 85
  Gladstone, W.E., 2
  Harris, "Bomber"
  Irving, Sir Henry, 31
  Lincoln, Abraham, 25
  Montgomery of Alamein, 101
  Myddelton, Sir Hugh, 133
  Palmerston, Lord, 27
  Peel, Robert, 27
  Raleigh, Sir Walter, 101
  Slim, Viscount, 101
  Smuts, Field Marshall Jan, 27
  Solomon, 80

Waterlow, Sir Sydney, 107
Wellington, 86
Stockwell,
  Memorial Clock Tower, 15
  Road, 15
Stoke Newington,
  Church Street, 114
  Town Hall, former, 114
  Water Works, 113
Stoll, Sir Oswald, Foundation, 68
Stratford,
  House, 75
  Place, 75
Street Markets
  Church Street, Marylebone/Paddington, 89
  Electric Avenue, Brixton, 15
  Green Park, Piccadilly (works of Art), 63
  Inverness Street, Camden Town, 104
Sullivan, Sir Arthur, 60, 103
Summerson, Sir John, 6
Surrey Commercial Docks, 9
Sussex Gardens, 73
Sutcliffe, Berkeley(designer), 62
Sutton, Jacob, 18

T

Tattersall's, 64
Temple Bar, 43, 80
Terminus Place, 14, 22
Thames Barrier, 130
Theatres
  Adelphi, Strand, 38, 40, 78
  Alcazar Music Hall, 60
  Aldwych, Aldwych, 38
  Apollo, Shaftesbury Avenue, 60
  Apollo Victoria, 14, 92
  Barbican, City, 79
  Cockpit, Downing Street, 100
  Collins Music Hall, Islington, 113
  Criterion, Piccadilly Circus, 76
  Dominion, Tottenham Court Road, 103
  Fortune, Russell Street, 39
  Garrick, Charing Cross Road, 102
  Gielgud (ex Globe), 60
  Globe (New), Southwark Haymarket, 147
  Her Majesty's, Haymarket, 34, 61, 76
  Hicks, 60
  Lyric, Shaftesbury Avenue, 60
  Moy's Music Hall, 85
  Old Vic, The Cut, Waterloo, 6
  Palace, Cambridge Circus, 60, 103
  Phoenix Charing Cross Road, 60, 103
  Queen's, Haymarket, 61
  Royal English Opera House, 60, 103
  Royal Opera, 39
  Royal Standard Music Hall, Pimlico, 85
  Sadlers Wells, Rosebery Avenue, 7
  Strand, Aldwych, 40, 78-79
  Theatre Royal Haymarket, 34, 61, 76
  Theatre Royal Marylebone, 89
  Vaudeville, Strand, 38, 78
  Victoria Palace, Victoria, 85, 93
  Wyndhams, Charing Cross Road, 102
"Theatres of London", 102

Theobalds Park, Hertfordshire, 43
Thomas Betterton's Company of Players, 61
Toc H (Talbot House), 83, 132
Toplady, The Rev'd Augustus, 34
Tourist Information Centres, 157
Tower Bridge Road, 8
Tower of London, 83, 14t3
Trafalgar. Battle of, 12, 77
Tritton, Sir Ernest, 19
Tulse Hill, 15
Turpin, "Dick"(highw), 106
"Two Roses", 78
Tyburn,
   Gate, 88
   tree, 73, 87
   Site, 88
   Way, 73

U

University College, London, 4
Upper York Place, 11

V

Vauxhall,
   Bridge Road, 14
   Pleasure Gardens, 14
Verulamium (St Albans), 88
Victoria Coach Station, 117
Victoria State Building, 2
Victoria Street, 22
Victory Club, Seymour Street, 8t1
Virgin & Child, Artillery Memorial, 13
Viroconium Cornoviorum (Wroxeter), 88
VISITORCALL, phone guide, 156

W

Wakefield, Edward Gibbon, 125
Walpole,
   Sir Horace, 29
   Sir Robert, 29, 42
Walsingham House, Piccadilly, 63
Warwick House Street, 34
Watch House, Oxford Street, 75
Waterloo,
   Battle of, 4, 15
   Churches, 6, 15
   Dinners, 87
   Road, 6, 7
Waterlow, Sir Sydney, 107
Watling Street, 73, 88
Watson, Doctor, 11, 35
Waye to Uxbridge, The, 73
Wellcome, Sir Henry, 110
Wellcome Institute, 110
Wellington, 58, 87
   Arch, 64, 86
   Monument (St Paul's), 47
Wesley, John, 104
West Norwood bus garage, 11
Westminster,
   City Council House, 125
   Hall, 7, 25
   Infirmary, 86

Temple of Apollo, 24
Whitefield, The Rev'd George, 104
Whitehall, 29
Whiteley, William, 122
Whittington,
   Richard "Dick", 108
   Stone, 108
Wig and Pen Restaurant (former Club), 43
Wilberforce, William(refmr), 87
Williams, George, 103
Wilson, Effingham, 5
Wilson, Harold (Lord Wilson of Rievaulx), 133
Wolfe Club, 42
WRENS, 3
Women's Royal Naval Service, 3
Wyndham, Charles, 102
Yeomen Warders, 83
Young Men s Christian Association
   (YMCA), 103
Young Women's Christian Association
   (YWCA), 103
"Youth", 41
Youth Hostel Association (YHA), 53

Also of Interest:

RAILWAY RAMBLES: London & the South-East

Clive Higgs, a lifelong Londoner who has always declined to own a car, describes a selection of attractive rambles that can be easily reached on the network of trains running from central London. **"Get down to the booking office now"** FARNHAM HERALD. £4.95

DOGS' LONDON

Twenty walks for London's dogs and their owners, all beginning and ending at tube or BR stations. Unrestricted runs for dogs and pleasant green scenery for their companions! Mary Scott and her dog, Fred, have personally tested every mile of these routes, many along little known paths that make such a change from the regular walk in the park! £6.95

BEST PUB WALKS IN AND AROUND CENTRAL LONDON

Discover London on foot, and pop into one or more of its famous hostelries. The pubs are packed with history and there's much to see on Ruth Herman's entertaining romp (and stagger?) around the streets of London. £6.95

All of our books are available from your local bookshop. In case of difficulty, or to obtain our complete catalogue, please contact: **Sigma Leisure, 1 South Oak Lane, Wilmslow, Cheshire SK9 6AR**
Phone: 01625 – 531035 Fax: 01625 – 536800   E-mail: sigma.press@zetnet.co.uk
ACCESS and VISA orders welcome. Please add £2 p&p to all orders.
Free Catalogue on request. Or see our catalogue on the web - http://www.sigmapress.co.uk